Nine Star Ki

Nine Star Ki

Michio Kushi's
Guidebook
on Love & Relationships,
Health & Travel
and Getting Through
the 1990s

By Michio Kushi
with Edward Esko

One Peaceful World Press
Becket, Massachusetts

Nine Star Ki
© 1991 by Michio Kushi and Edward Esko

Published by One Peaceful World, Becket, Mass.

For information on mail-order sales, wholesale or retail discounts, distribution, translations, and foreign rights, please contact the publishers:

One Peaceful World Press
Box 10
Becket, Mass. 01223
U.S.A.
(413) 623-5742

First edition: February 1991
10 9 8 7 6 5 4 3 2 1

ISBN: 0-9628528-0-5

Printed in U.S.A.

Contents

List of Tables and Charts

Introduction

I first heard Michio Kushi lecture in the spring of 1971 at the Friends' Meeting House in Philadelphia. His basic message — that living in harmony with nature could open the door to an era of planetary health and peace — resonated with my own thoughts and feelings. He stated that humanity's destination was one peaceful world and offered a simple roadmap for getting there. After hearing the lecture, I realized that I shared a similar view of the future.

Soon afterward I moved to Boston. In those days, Boston was the hub of the worldwide macrobiotic community. Michio would lecture three or four nights a week and sometimes on weekends. He presented an incredible range of topics — from spiritual development to future world government, from Oriental diagnosis to the evolution of consciousness, and from the teachings of Lao Tzu to the teachings of Jesus — all in a new and original way. Students came from all over the world to participate in the excitement of endless new discovery.

Of all the subjects that Michio introduced, Oriental astrology — and especially Nine Star Ki — continues to be one of the most popular. Originating thousands of years ago in the Far East, Nine Star Ki provides an accurate guide to the movement of life energy, or ki, in nature and human affairs. Derived from the law of endless change, it sheds light on past events and future probabilities and is surprisingly accurate in predicting individual and social destiny.

The material in this guidebook is an introduction to what

is actually an endless field of study and is based on lectures given by Michio over the past decade, including his annual Predictions Seminars at the end of every year. It offers insight into the invisible forces that shape human events, with practical suggestions on love and relationships, health, psychology, and travel, together with discussions of world events and guidelines for charting a safe passage into the 21st century.

Since introducing Nine Star Ki in the West, Michio has continued to broaden its application. A variety of new applications were added in the new Destiny and Spiritual Training Development Seminars that he now gives in Becket. Readers who would like up-to-date information on Nine Star Ki are encouraged to attend these ongoing programs presented at the Kushi Institute of the Berkshires.

I would like to thank everyone who assisted in producing this edition. I thank Gale Jack for copyediting and proofreading the text and offering many helpful suggestions, as well as for reprinting several questions and answers from her column on Nine Star Ki, that appears regularly in the *One Peaceful World Newsletter*. I also thank Alex Jack for overseeing the final production and thank Karen Claffey, Dennis Shepard, and Elizabeth Erb for their production assistance. I also thank my wife, Wendy, for her help and support, Herb Shapiro for his support and encouragement, and the staffs of *Order of the Universe* and *One Peaceful World*, where some of this material was originally published, for their editorial assistance.

Edward Esko
Becket, Massachusetts
November, 1990

Part I

Oriental Astrology in Love, Health, and Relationships

Historical Background

The principles of Oriental astrology and the macrobiotic way of life are actually one and the same. They were established many thousands of years ago in a highly developed, spiritually oriented civilization that encompassed the entire planet. Originally, macrobiotics was not a system of diet or health, but first arose as a unified cosmology, or universal philosophy. This philosophy was subsequently applied to all domains of human activity and understanding, eventually including the study and practice of proper diet and good health.

Oriental Astrology, including Nine Star Ki, developed as a part of this universal cosmology. Actually, the title "Oriental" is somewhat of a misnomer, as the ancients who developed this system were not confined to one geographic area, but traveled widely throughout the globe. It was only as a later development, following a series of world-scale catastrophes that caused this ancient one-world civilization to collapse, that people on earth became divided and isolated into separate territories and cultures.

After that time, from 10,000 to 12,000 years ago, this original cosmology and its various applications survived in differing forms throughout all the surviving, independent ancient cultures, but they have remained in a form closest to their original in the Far East. This entire development is well recorded in the ancient historical documents of Japan and China.

In ancient China, according to legend, there were three great emperors, each of whom made a contribution to our understanding of the order of the universe. The first of these, called Fu Hi, is credited with first formulating the language of yin and yang in describing the interactions and changing processes of all things. He expressed these polar tendencies as a broken line (- -) for yin, and a solid line (–) for yang, and combined these two symbols to create eight trigrams or stages of change.

With this very simple system, Fu Hi was able to accurately describe the primary stages in the universal cycle of change that governs all things, from atoms to galaxies. Later, Fu Hi's eight trigrams were expanded into 64 hexagrams, and this description of the universal cycle of change became the basis for the *I Ching*, or "Book of Changes."

The second emperor, Shin No, developed this understanding further and applied yin and yang to the world of food and agriculture. The literal meaning of "Shin No" is "divine agriculture." In the process of studying the life cycle of cereal grains and other plants, Shin No naturally became interested in developing a more detailed understanding of seasonal, planetary, and celestial influences. Working with these natural influences is very important in the practice of farming. This was the origin of the various systems of astrology described below.

The third emperor was Ko Tei, or the "Yellow Emperor," who carried these accomplishments one step further. His deepening study of plants and agriculture resulted in a comprehensive understanding of food and its effects on the body, while his application of Shin No's understanding of cosmology and celestial motion to the human body itself produced a new understanding of our meridians and ki flow, eventually creating the techniques of Oriental medicine, including acupuncture and massage.

The studies of the three emperors progressed from a more yin, abstract form with Fu Hi to more tangible applications with Shin No (the energy of stars, seasons, and plants), and finally to the study of the human body and its relationship to the environment. Over the intervening millennia, humanity has gradually lost its sensitivity to the world of vibration, as we have become more concerned with material development and as our biological conditions have become more clouded and insensitive.

Recently, however, many people have begun to eat a more simple, clean diet based on whole cereal grains, beans, vegetables, sea vegetables, and other complex carbohydrate foods. This way of eating is very close to that of these ancient wise leaders, and as we continue to eat this way our conditions, perceptions, mentality, and view of life are coming into closer alignment with those ancient conditions and views. As we gradually refine our ability to directly sense the huge world of vibrations, our perceptions and interests are naturally progressing from the most yang manifestations, like acupuncture, shiatsu, food, and health, to more yin manifestations, such as the perception of celestial influence, the spiritual world, and an intuitive grasp of the origin and meaning of life.

The Five Transformations

In order to understand how Oriental astrology works, we need to have a clear comprehension of the patterns of movement and change that govern all things on earth. Ancient thinkers observed nature and saw that all things continually pass through alternating stages of contraction and expansion, and within this universal process, they discerned five archetypal phases, or stages of transformation. These five stages can be summarized as: (1) ascending, rapidly expanding energy, or "tree" nature; (2) very expanded, highly activated "free" energy, or "fire" nature; (3) gathering, condensing, downward and inward moving energy, or "soil" nature; (4) fully consolidated, materialized energy, or "metal" nature; and (5) slowly dissolving, floating energy on the borderline between strong condensation and strong expansion, or "water" nature.

These five stages are shown in *Figure 1*, together with the times of day, times of year, and major body organs with which they are associated. Viewing the complete cycle of five stages as one continuous process, you can see that this

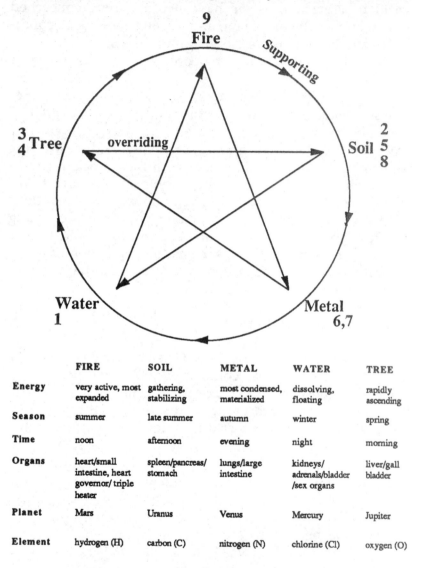

Figure 1: The Five Transformations

	FIRE	SOIL	METAL	WATER	TREE
Energy	very active, most expanded	gathering, stabilizing	most condensed, materialized	dissolving, floating	rapidly ascending
Season	summer	late summer	autumn	winter	spring
Time	noon	afternoon	evening	night	morning
Organs	heart/small intestine, heart governor/ triple heater	spleen/pancreas/ stomach	lungs/large intestine	kidneys/ adrenals/bladder /sex organs	liver/gall bladder
Planet	Mars	Uranus	Venus	Mercury	Jupiter
Element	hydrogen (H)	carbon (C)	nitrogen (N)	chlorine (Cl)	oxygen (O)

is simply a more detailed view of yin and yang, with soil and metal energy representing the phase of contraction, and water, tree, and fire energy representing the phase of expansion. For example, the seasons of late summer and fall comprise an overall more condensing time of year, while from the deep winter through summer, the atmosphere is as a whole expanding.

Because of this overall continuous sequence, it is easy to see that each stage naturally supports or produces the energy of the following stage: soil energy creates and supports metal energy, which in turn gives birth to and reinforces water energy, which creates and nourishes tree energy, and so forth. This sequential relationship is called the *Shen Cycle*, or "cycle of creation," and the relation of each stage to the next is called the "parent/child" relationship.

The other basic interrelation to consider is that of each energy stage to those stages lying at the opposite half of the cycle. When the gathering, consolidating energy of soil nature is emphasized, naturally the opposite, dissolving or dispersing energy of water nature is inhibited. When water nature energy is encouraged, the more energetic, active stage of fire nature is suppressed. Fire nature energy, in turn, tends to cancel out or prevent the heavily materializing energy of metal nature; and so forth. This cycle of suppression or control is often called the *Ko Cycle*.

There are also many associations with these five stages, such as different times of day, seasons, body organs, planets and chemical elements that represent each type of energy. The planet Venus, for example, has the strongest influence on the earth during a metal period. This period is also characterized by autumn or evening phenomena, with particular emphasis on the lungs and large intestine, and the element nitrogen. At the same time, this influence overrides the influence of Jupiter, which is called *Moku Sei*, or "tree star," in the Far East. During a time of water nature we are particularly influenced by the planet Mercury, by deep night or mid-winter types of energy conditions, the energies of the kidneys, bladder, adrenals and sex organs, and the element chlorine.

19

Once you have clearly grasped the dynamic behavior of yin and yang, of their more detailed manifestations in the five transformations, and the common sense, vivid logic of these *Shen* and *Ko* relationships, you can easily understand all of ancient and Oriental thought, including ancient Oriental astrology. To put it another way, if you don't understand yin and yang and the five transformations, it is impossible to really understand any of these ancient, traditional ways of thinking.

Ten Heavenly Influences (*Ji Kan*)

Japanese Name	Short Nam	English Translation	Description of Meaning	Recent Years
Ki No E	Ko	Tree Elder	Beginning of plants (seeds)	1984
Ki No To	Otsu	Tree Younger	Beginning of buds	1985
Hi No E	Hei	Fire Elder	Sprouts	1986
Hi No To	Tei	Fire Younger	Rapid growth of young branches	1987
Tsuchi No E	Bo	Soil Elder	Growth of leaves and twigs	1988
Tsuchi No To	Ki	Soil Younger	Extreme growth (zenith)	1989
Ka No E	Ko	Metal Elder	Withering begins	1990
Ka No To	Shin	Metal Younger	Leaves falling down	1991
Mizu No E	Jin	Water Elder	Implantation of seeds	1992
Mizu No To	Ki	Water Younger	Waiting until spring (dormancy)	1993

Figure 2: Table of Ten Heavenly Influences

The great current of celestial energy raining down on the earth passes through a cycle of alternating greater force and lesser force, within which five distinct stages can be felt. These five stages are called *Ki* (tree), *Hi* (fire), *Tsuchi* (soil), *Ka* (metal) and *Mizu* (water). Each of these stages, in turn, passes through an early phase and later phase, called *E* (elder brother or beginning) and *To* (younger brother or ending), producing a total sequence of ten different phases. These are listed in *Figure 2* with their full names, shortened names, and English translations.

These ten phases are further associated with ten stages of growth and decay, as exemplified in the yearly cycle of vegetation, providing the *Ji Kan* system with the vividly practical imagery of the agricultural year. In actual use, these ten progressions are applied to cycles of both ten days each, and of ten years each, so that each specific day and each specific year has its own particular quality within this ten-fold process.

In terms of human destiny, this cycle of heavenly energy influences our mind, thinking, personality, and character. It also influences our growth and development, particularly the development of our intellect and spirituality and capacity to receive vibrations. In terms of natal characteristics, a person's particular *Ji Kan* qualities are transmitted through the father and the father's reproductive cells and most strongly influence the quality of the brain and nervous and respiratory systems.

For example, 1990 was a metal elder brother (*Ka No E*) year. In that year there was a subtle influence that caused us to tend toward more conservative, practical, tangible or material types of thinking and character, the vibrational influence of Venus was influential, and the autumn/evening quality gave us the tendency toward times of quiet, serious, even melancholic reflection.

Twelve Earthly Influences (*Ju Ni Shi*)

Animal Name	Zodiac	Month	Hour	Year	Meridian
Rat	Aquarius	Jan-Feb	11pm-1am	1984, 1996	gall bladder
Cow	Pisces	Feb-Mar	1-3 am	1985, 1997	liver
Tiger	Aries	Mar-Apr	3-5 am	1986, 1998	lung
Rabbit	Taurus	Apr-May	5-7 am	1987, 1999	large intestine
Dragon	Gemini	May-Jun	7-9 am	1988, 2000	stomach
Snake	Cancer	Jun-Jul	9-11 am	1989, 2001	spleen
Horse	Leo	Jul-Aug	11am-1pm	1990, 2002	heart
Sheep	Virgo	Aug-Sept	1-3 pm	1991, 2003	small intestine
Monkey	Libra	Sept-Oct	3-5 pm	1992, 2004	bladder
Rooster	Scorpio	Oct-Nov	5-7 pm	1993, 2005	kidney
Dog	Sagitarius	Nov-Dec	7-9 pm	1994, 2006	heart govenor
Boar	Capricorn	Dec-Jan	9-11 pm	1995, 2007	triple heater

Figure 3: Correlations of the Twelve
Earthly Influences

Within the constant stream of centrifugal energy radiating out from the earth, there are again regular fluctuations, occurring in a cycle of twelve. These twelve stages of more horizontal energy, or earthly influence, are already familiar to most of you through their association with the twelve constellations of the Zodiac. They also correlate to the approximately twelve-year revolution of Jupiter around the sun (Jupiter, the largest planet in the solar system, represents tree nature energy, which is due to its rapidly expanding, ascending character, and correlates to the earth's centrifugal energy upon which this twelve-year cycle is based); and to the recurring cycle of sunspot peaks and lows.

In addition, the twelve constellations of the Zodiac themselves strongly correlate to the twelve major body organs and meridians of ki energy. In Oriental medicine

Popular Name	Sound	Original Character	Meaning (original)
Rat	Ne	Hitone	Seed, roots
Cow	Usi	Fukuramu	Swelling, taking in water
Tiger	Tora	Toake	Opening, coming out
Rabbit	U	Umare	Birth
Dragon	Tatsu	Tatsuru	Standing up
Snake	Mi	Minori	Fruits
Horse	Uma	Umami	Delicious (ripe fruits)
Sheep	Hitsuji	Trotori	Colorful
Monkey	Saru	Tori	Taking in, harvest
Rooster	Tori	Torihiniri	Appreciate, sorting harvest
Dog	Inu	Irabu	Choosing (new seeds)
Boar	I	Iruoru	Storing (dormancy)

Figure 4: Origin of Animal Names for the Twelve Years

there are twelve two-hour periods of the day during which each individual organ and meridian is most actively influenced by one of those Zodiacal signs, as well as twelve months in the year with the same associations. These times are often used in acupuncture and other forms of natural healing for their particular effects.

This cycle of twelve stages also applies to periods of twelve years, which are again more popular in the form of Chinese astrology, with its animal names for the twelve years (Year of the Tiger, Year of the Dragon, etc.). However, like the *Ten Kan*, these twelve progressions were also originally associated with twelve stages of growth and decay in the yearly cycle of the cereal plant. Then about 3,000 years ago, as both the domestication of animals and the consumption of animal foods became more widespread, these twelve stages were popularized for everyday use by a very clever method: ancient Chinese astronomers chose twelve animals whose characters somewhat matched those twelve stages of energy change, and whose Chinese names were phonetically similar to the more ancient agricultural names. Both versions are presented here.

In practical use, you can retain the more ancient agricultural names or adopt the more modern animal names. Since the latter are more familiar, and to help avoid confusion between the twelve divisions of earthly influence and the ten progressions of heavenly influence, I will use the animal names.

While we can describe these periods in terms of the twelve-month year, bear in mind that the same twelve traits are exhibited over twelve years, giving a person born in a certain year a general quality that we can associate with the corresponding month. Babies born during 1990, for example, which is a Horse year, will have a certain summerlike aspect to their personality. Let's see how this works in more detail.

The Twelve Natal Characteristics

We can divide the year into two opposite, complementary halves: cold weather and warm weather. People who pass through the nine months of pregnancy during the warmer months, when the mother is eating generally more yin food such as salad or fruit, are born with a more yin constitution during the autumn and winter. Those who are carried through the autumn and winter, while the mother is eating more yang food such as cooked foods, salty foods, and more animal foods, are born with a more yang constitution some time in the spring or summer. The borderline between these two types of people is generally about mid-March (Tiger) and mid-September (Monkey).

Those people born during the spring and summer, the

Physical Development	Mental Development
TIGER March 1986 planning initiative	MONKEY September 1992 planning, initiative
RABBIT April 1987 beginning to move	ROOSTER October 1993 beginning to move
DRAGON May 1988 active development, opening out	DOG November 1994 active development
SNAKE June 1989 adaptation, flexibility (MOST YANG)	BOAR December 1995 adaptibility, application (MOST YIN)
HORSE July 1990 differentiation	RAT January 1996 differentiation
SHEEP August 1991 slowing down	COW February 1997 slowing down, dormancy

Figure 5: Natal Characteristics of the Twelve Years

more yang category, generally have a more active, outgoing, physical and social nature, while those born in the autumn or winter, the more yin category, generally have a more inward, quiet, mental character, and tend to be thinking types rather than doing types.

People born at the beginning of the more physical time (Tiger/March) tend to be good at making plans, especially plans for social or physical development. They may not themselves carry those plans out, but the initial planning ability is very good. In the next stage, Rabbit/April-born people begin to move on those plans. Dragon/May-born people give those plans further, more active development,

24

bringing them more out into the open. Snake/June-born people are the most active, yang type, carrying out these plans with very active, practical, and adaptive motion. Snake type people are generally very flexible, and this is also said to be a sign of great beauty in women. The movements of a Snake person, however, may tend to become a little unstable and poorly directed, and this tendency increases with Horse/July-born people, who tend to change jobs, activities, and directions often, with very branched out, differentiated movement. This activity slows down markedly during the August/Sheep time, so that while Horse-born people are usually very active, Sheep-born people are usually more quiet and gentle, something like an actual sheep.

Then the period of physical motion ends and the more introspective, mental period begins. Here again, Monkey/September-born people lead the way with the planning stage—planning in some more mental, intellectual, or theoretical field. Although this is one of the more yin types, don't forget that the original meaning of Monkey was to harvest or take in, and this is still a fairly active character. Monkey-born people tend to have very active, agile minds and very humorous, clever personalities, something like a monkey. Then again, Rooster/October-born people begin to move on these plans, and this development grows further with Dog/November-born people. Mental flexibility and adaptability comes more with Boar/December-born people, as well as more actual application on those ideas in various circumstances. With Rat/January-born people, this mental activity becomes again very differentiated and even scattered, and then begins to slow down and go into dormancy with Cow/February-born people. It is interesting the Cow and Sheep are opposite each other, yet both represent more slowing down types.

1991 is a Sheep year; 1990 was a Horse year, and 1989 was a Snake year, and so forth. Using the table in *Figure 6*, please see in what type of year you were born, and find out what constitutional type you yourself represent.

One important point: this twelve-month year is consid-

Rat	1900	1912	1924	1936	1948	1960	1972	1984	1996
Cow	01	13	25	37	49	61	73	85	97
Tiger	02	14	26	38	50	62	74	86	98
Rabbit	03	15	27	39	51	63	75	87	99
Dragon	04	16	28	40	52	64	76	88	2000
Snake	05	17	29	41	53	65	77	89	01
Horse	06	18	30	42	54	66	78	90	02
Sheep	07	19	31	43	55	67	79	91	03
Monkey	08	20	32	44	56	68	80	92	04
Rooster	09	21	33	45	57	69	81	93	05
Dog	10	22	34	46	58	70	82	94	06
Boar	11	23	35	47	59	71	83	95	07

**Figure 6: Twelve Energy Correlations
with Years in the 20th Century**

ered to begin on about February 4th. That is, if you were born before February 4th of a certain year, consider yourself as having been born during the previous year. So, for example, all babies born between February 4th, 1990, and February 3rd, 1991, are Horse-year children.

In addition to these twelve types and those two categories of six types each, ancient astrologers also found certain common characteristics within each sequence of three consecutive stages. Since there are four sets of three months each, this produces the classification of three energy types each with four members shown in *Figure 7*. *O Ki* means very active energy, *Bo Ki* means sinking or diminishing energy, and *Sei Ki* means rising or increasing energy. Every three years, every three months, and every six hours (three two-hour periods) the earth's energy passes through this sequence of high activity, sinking energy, and rising energy.

People born under an *O Ki* sign (Rat, Rabbit, Horse, Rooster) as a whole tend to be more active, outgoing, and energetic, more talkative and physical or action-oriented, and tend not to enjoy more calm, reflective, or yin activities. People born under a *Bo Ki* sign (Cow, Dragon, Sheep, Dog) are generally more inward-turning and reflective, as well as more thoughtful and mentally oriented. People born under a *Sei Ki* sign (Tiger, Snake, Monkey, Boar) tend to be more optimistic, idealistic or romantic, pursuing romantic images and dreams. In a word, we can summarize these three general types as: practical (*O Ki*), self-reflective (*Bo Ki*) and idealistic (*Sei Ki*). Of course, their dispersal

O KI – active energy	BO KI – sinking energy	SEI KI – rising energy
Physically & socially active	Reflective, thoughtful, practical	Romantic, idealistic, optimistic
Rat	Cow	Tiger
Rabbit	Dragon	Snake
Horse	Sheep	Monkey
Rooster	Dog	Boar

**Figure 7: The Three-Year Pattern
of Natal Characteristics**

throughout the twelve-year cycle gives each member of each group its own distinct interpretation of that general quality.

In terms of human destiny, this cycle of earthly energy influences more the quality of our material body and outward, immediate personality, transmitted at conception and throughout pregnancy primarily through our mother and mother's reproductive cells, and more strongly influencing the quality of our digestive, circulatory, and reproductive systems.

Heaven, Earth, and Humanity

In summary, the ten progressions of heaven's energy create our spiritual, mental, and emotional tendencies, while the twelve branches of earth's order create our physical, material, and social tendencies. Altogether, this represents a total of 120 different possible basic atmospheric conditions. Furthermore, these 120 different conditions can combine in a multitude of different yearly, monthly, daily and hourly combinations. From the study of these many, many different types of situations and their various inter-relations, the study of Oriental astrology began.

However, for practical use, ancient people discovered a third, more comprehensive system, which represents a synthesis of these two. In between heaven's order and earth's order, there is the human order, so they classified phenomena under the terms of Heaven, Earth, and Humanity. Or to say it another way, celestial influence plus the earth's influence produces the atmosphere, sperm and egg produce the embryo, father and mother create children, and the ten heavenly progressions of active energy plus the twelve earthly branches of passive energy produce nine energy changes. In the ancient Orient, this third method was called *Kyu Sei Ki Gaku*, or "Nine Star Ki Study."

Nine Star Ki

The most comprehensive of ancient astrological systems, Nine Star Ki Study is based on a recurring cycle of nine distinct atmospheric conditions. Over the course of nine years – also every nine months and also every nine days – the earth's atmosphere regularly passes through the nine stages or energy levels shown in *Figure 8*. In modern times, the outermost planets of Neptune, Uranus, and Pluto were discovered only within the past several hundred years, but thousands of years ago, Oriental astronomers were intimately familiar with all nine planets and recognized that the vibrational influence of each one ruled one of these nine stages. These were the nine "stars." Furthermore, the nine stages correlate to nine constellations over the north pole, where vibrational influence on the earth is particularly strong.

Each stage is assigned a number, from 1 through 9. According to the individual level of energy, each stage is also grouped within one of the five transformations. This association is easy to see: the highest, most active energy level is considered fire nature, and this is also the number 9, the

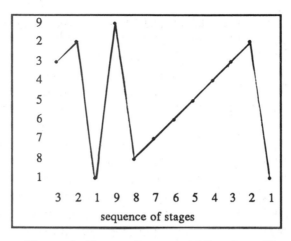

most expanded or yin number. On the opposite side, the lowest, most inactive energy is classified as water nature, with the most yang, contracted number 1. In the exact middle, the number 5 identifies the most balanced or intermediate level of energy, the halfway point between 1 and 9. This is classified as soil nature, soil being generally the stage of balance.

Stages 3 and 4 are both of relatively higher energy levels, and correlate to the rising energy of spring, morning, and tree nature. Stages 6 and 7 represent lower, more dense or contracted energy levels, corresponding to autumn, evening, and metal nature. In between the extreme low of number 1 and the rising energy of 3 and 4, number 2 represents a smaller-scale stage of balance, also being classified as soil nature. Likewise, the number 8 mediates the transition from the dense levels of 6 and 7 to the extremely active, expanded energy of number 9, and is also classified as soil nature.

In terms of the seasons of the year, ancient people actually observed four different soil nature periods, representing four transitional stages between each season and the next. As the influence of each season wanes and begins to transform into the next, a period of approximately 18 days and 6 hours occurs as a time of stability or soil nature.

	Color	Nature	ement	Direction	Trigram	Attributes	Years
9	Purple	Fire	H	S	Li	Middle Daughter, clarity	1991
8	White	Soil	C	NE	Ken	Youngest Son, mountain, keeping still	1992
7	Red	Metal	N	W	Tui	Youngest Daughter, lake, joyousness	1993
6	White	Metal	N	NW	Ch'ien	Father, creative, heaven	1994
5	Yellow	Soil	C	Center	none		1995
4	Dark Green	Tree	O	SE	Sun	Eldest Daughter, penetration, wind	1996
3	Bright Green	Tree	O	E	Chen	Eldest Son, arousing, thunder	1997
2	Black	Soil	C	SW	K'un	Mother, receptive, earth	1998
1	White	Water	Cl	N	K'an	Middle Son, river, danger	1999

Figure 9: Nine Star Ki Correlations

While the number 5 relates to all four of these periods in general, the slightly more expansive level of number 2 relates more to the end of summer before the contraction of autumn, and the number 8 relates more to the cold latter part of winter before the first stirring of spring.

The nine stages are also associated with nine symbolic colors, with various elements (by the same classification given before) and, with the exception of number 5, with the eight trigrams of Fu Hi, upon which the hexagrams of the *I Ching* are based. In *Figure 9*, these correlations are all shown together with examples of several recent yearly cycles.

While the cycle of ten (*Ji Kan*) has particular influence on our more mental, vibrational development, and the cycle of twelve (*Ju Ni Shi*) influences more outward appearances and material development, the Nine Star Ki cycle has a pervading, overall influence on all aspects of our lives. For example, the economy expanded actively during the Tree years of 1987 and 1988 and started to turn downward during 1989, which was a more stabilizing 2 Soil year. 1990 was a 1 Water year, a time of floating, slowly moving energy, and economic stagnation accelerated, bankruptcies occurred on Wall Street, and the economy slid into a recession.

As the years progress forward, the Nine Star numbers progress backward, going from 9 to 1, or from yin to yang. This is because in our present epoch we are generally following a yang, materializing spiral. Please think this over, and try to figure out when in the future this direction will reverse and begin going from 1 up to 9, or in other words, when a new, spiritually oriented civilization will begin. The months each also have their own energy nature, and these numbers are also progressing backward, going from 9 to 1. This direction also changes in larger cycles and will reverse in the future. The monthly cycle reverses direction much more frequently than the yearly cycle. Can you figure out how many years it takes for this cycle to change direction?

Each day also has a different energy, and the daily cycle reverses direction twice a year, following the general energy of the seasons. From about the time of the winter solstice to about the time of the summer solstice, or from December to June, the earth's atmospheric energy is gradually becoming more active and expanded, and earth's force is generally stronger. During this half of the year, the daily numbers ascend from 1 to 9. In June, near the time of the summer solstice, the expansion of earth's force peaks and heaven's force gradually begins to assert dominance; the number 9 repeats, and the series reverses direction to descend from 9 to 1 until the winter solstice. In Oriental terminology, they call these two processes *Yin Ton* and *Yang*

Calendar Month	Nature	Actual Month
January (1991)	6 White Metal	1/5 - 2/3
February	5 Yellow Soil	2/4 - 3/5
March	4 Green Tree	3/6 - 4/4
April	3 Green Tree	4/5 - 5/4
May	2 Black Soil	5/5 - 6/5
June	1 White Water	6/6 - 7/6
July	9 Purple Fire	7/7 - 8/6
August	8 White Soil	8/7 - 9/7
September	7 Red Metal	9/8 - 10/7
October	6 White Metal	10/8 - 11/6
November	5 Yellow Soil	11/7 - 12/6
December	4 Green Tree	12/7 - 1/4
January (1992)	3 Green Tree	1/5 - 2/3
February	2 Black Soil	2/4 - 3/5

Figure 10: Nine Star Ki Months for 1991 and 1992

Ton. (The word "ton" means "process.")

Each day also has correspondences with the *Ten Kan* and *Twelve Shi* systems. Combining all three characters for any given day, month, or year, you can form a considerably detailed image of the precise nature of vibration or context within which the events of the period will happen. According to this image, you can begin to reasonably predict the general tendency of your own life, human events around you, regional or national events, even the weather and atmospheric events. In other words, all motion, all change, and all events in the vicinity of the earth are integrally linked with this matrix of vibrational influences.

Each of these three has a somewhat distinct, unique influence: the *Ten Kan* provides a more emotional, psychological, and spiritual influence, while the *Twelve Shi* influences more the actual events, physical movement, and activity of that period. In different terms, we can say these represent the more subjective and more objective aspects of that day, month, or year. The Nine Star Ki character and influence provides a general, synthesized description of that

32

period's atmospheric quality, manifesting as the average or underlying background of those appearances.

In terms of priorities, you can first consider the qualities of the year, then of the month, and then of the day, going from most pervasive, overall influence to most superficial, immediate influence. Also, Nine Star Ki is the most important factor determining the overall character and outcomes of that day, month or year; *Ten Kan* is second, and *Twelve Shi* is third.

Nine Star Ki Year Qualities

Looking at the table in *Figure 11*, please determine the Nine Star Ki nature of your own year of birth. This is your own constitutional nature. When making this determination, please note that the Nine Star Ki year actually begins not on January 1 but on February 4. This represents the half-way point between the winter solstice and the spring equinox. If you were born before that date, consider yourself as belonging to the previous year – for example, people born between January 1 and February 3, 1991, will not be 9 Fire people, but 1 Water people.

Now, using just the year of birth by Nine Star Ki, let's look at these nine constitutional types, one by one.

• **1 White Water** – This color is not really white, but more transparent like water; a person born under this sign has a more "transparent" personality, in that he or she can very freely, flexibly adapt himself or herself to any other personality or situation. This character is usually easygoing and agreeable, often involved in writing or some form of communication and creative work. If this person becomes too weak, that adaptability can grow extreme to the point of being noncommittal, indecisive, and lacking in clear opinions or direction.

Although 1 Water people appear gentle and reserved on the surface, inside they are strong. They are good listeners, but often don't reveal their true feelings, and are good at keeping secrets. One Waters have clear insight and are able

9	Fire	1901	1910	1919	1928	1937	1946	1955	1964	1973	1982	1991	2000
8	Soil	1902	1911	1920	1929	1938	1947	1956	1965	1974	1983	1992	2001
7	Metal	1903	1912	1921	1930	1939	1948	1957	1966	1975	1984	1993	2002
6	Metal	1904	1913	1922	1931	1940	1949	1958	1967	1976	1985	1994	2003
5	Soil	1905	1914	1923	1932	1941	1950	1959	1968	1977	1986	1995	2004
4	Tree	1906	1915	1924	1933	1942	1951	1960	1969	1978	1987	1996	2005
3	Tree	1907	1916	1925	1934	1943	1952	1961	1970	1979	1988	1997	2006
2	Soil	1908	1917	1926	1935	1944	1953	1962	1971	1980	1989	1998	2007
1	Water	1909	1918	1927	1936	1945	1954	1963	1972	1981	1990	1999	2008

Figure 11: Nine Star Ki Correlations with Years in the 20th Century

to see the front and back of situations. In conversation, they are sensitive to other peoples' feelings and tend to adapt their responses accordingly. Their judgment is often clear and their actions deliberate, and they make good leaders.

One Waters are good at social relations. They care for others but inside may harbor feelings of superiority. They like having a pond on their property or an aquarium in their home. People born under this sign are usually very interested in the opposite sex and may have many love affairs. However, they are discreet and keep their personal lives confidential. They are often successful in founding an enterprise or business.

Typical Occupations: Philosopher, lawyer, politician, writer, thinker, doctor, manager of a fish or seafood business, printer, manager of a restaurant or coffee shop, expert on natural fermentation, painter, manager of a public bath, entertainer, bookstore manager, gas station operator.

• **2 Black Soil** – All three of the soil nature types are of a generally balanced, centered, stabilized character. People born under these signs are usually more secure and thoughtful. Soil number 2 is the more yin of the three soils, and people born under this sign are more outgoing and social, easily becoming interested in music, culture, philosophy, politics, business, or any social field. In the extreme, this nurturing, fertile energy can become too idealistic and a little impractical.

Two Soil people have very sincere natures, and usually achieve success through the slow, steady accumulation of effort. Success tends to come later in life. They can be overly sensitive and have difficulty adapting to sudden change. Two Soils don't open their hearts easily and tend to prefer solitude. They sometimes pay too much attention to detail and have the tendency to be perfectionists. Two Soil people sometimes make demands of others and can be pushy when stating their opinions. Their conversations tend to revolve around work, and they don't like to waste time.

Two Soil people are able to devote themselves to the needs of others. They tend to procrastinate, and often choose 7 Metal people for husbands or wives. Their work tends to revolve around one project or area which they pursue with full vitality. They do better in professional careers than in organizations. Their perfectionist tendencies cause them to prefer doing things themselves rather than delegating responsibility to others.

Typical Occupations: Farmer, construction engineer, real estate broker, manager of a general store, educator, caterer, restaurant manager, women's fashion designer, manager of an antique store, porcelain trader, director of a charitable organization.

• **3 Bright Green Tree** – Both 3 and 4 represent spring type personalities: very emotional, poetic, idealistic types, with an eye on very long-range goals and more aesthetic or spiritual values. Between the two, number 3 is more brilliant and active, full of energy and curiosity. In the extreme, this character can easily overlook the more practical aspects of life and tend toward superficial thinking.

Three Tree people sometimes act before thinking, and many have quick tempers. However, 3 Trees are often kind- hearted. Their feelings tend to show immediately in their facial expressions, and their faces often become flushed. They are clear about what their likes and dislikes are, and stick to their opinions. They express themselves in a straightforward manner and have difficulty lying. Other people sometimes see them as opinionated or strong-willed.

Many 3 Trees have some type of secret that they are afraid of revealing. They have quick minds and like being the best at whatever they do. They tend to respect their fathers, and are considerate of their elders. They have strong romantic tendencies and are often attracted to someone who is pursuing an idealistic dream. They dislike monotony in their work, yet it is to their advantage to devote themselves to a single project or endeavor. Three Tree people often achieve fame or success before the age of 30. If they work in an organization, they tend to be promoted quickly, and are often financially successful.

Typical Occupations: Electrician, communications specialist, musician, composer, singer, computer expert, master of ceremonies, surgeon, army marshal, martial arts expert, politician, journalist, explorer, inventor, forester.

• **4 Dark Green Tree** – This represents the green of older, more matured growth. Those born during this year tend to be more thoughtful and practical, and to manifest their idealism in less romantic, more ambitious, or socially oriented goals.

The symbol for this sign is a large, mature tree. Four Tree people are generally of two types. People in the first group are more subdued and have great powers of analysis and strong theoretical ability. They make excellent philosophers, scientists, or administrators, and their contributions are often appreciated by society. Many Nobel Prize winners are among this category. Those in the second category are sensitive to other people's feelings and can embrace many different views. They are idealistic but often lose sight of practicalities, and have a tendency to waste time, energy, and money. Both 4 Tree types have a strong desire for freedom and justice, and this can lead them to resist established authority. They are usually eloquent and have the ability to agitate or influence other people. However, they are often indecisive and tend to go along with majority opinion and regret it later. Four Trees often have a hearty laugh and pat other people on the back.

People born under this sign are active in romance. Many 4 Tree men are playboy types. They frequently suffer because of love and tend to get married either very early or very late. They may take financial risks and experience financial insecurity. Four Trees are attracted to administration and management, but are usually disinterested in operational details. They are better at being advisors and guiding the overall direction of an enterprise rather than getting involved with the details of organization.

Typical Occupations: Importer/exporter, carpenter, craftsman, folk artist, salesperson, travel agent, broadcaster, publisher, film producer, television director, advertising executive, warehouser, stockbroker, manager of a noodle shop, manager of a general store, fabric designer, textile manufacturer.

• **5 Yellow Soil** – Yellow being the most balanced color of the spectrum, the energy of this year expresses the highest degree of balance between the extremes of water and fire. People born during a number 5 year tend to have very clear, well-defined opinions and character, often automatically becoming the center of every relationship, business enterprise or community in which they participate. Five Yellow Soil people tend to be surrounded by many people who grow to depend on them for objective viewpoints and clear, direct, impartial guidance. Since they are usually so clear and well-respected, these people may in the extreme have a tendency to become self-important, opinionated, or egotistical.

Five Soil people are gentle on the outside and strong inside. They are realistic, practical types who tend to dislike pointless discussions. They think things out before acting and then proceed step by step. Their opinions are strongly held, and they don't change their minds easily. They sometimes have difficulty adapting to new situations. Five Soils have a strong appetite for knowledge and like to study and do research. They enjoy history, reading, and hobbies and spending time quietly reflecting. Their strong confidence, vitality, and independence can make it difficult for them to work as part of a team. They like challenges and new ideas and have tremendous willpower.

Five Soils are good at taking responsibility and prefer to solve their personal problems by themselves. They have the strength and vitality to create a new life under any circumstance. Their self-confidence sometimes makes them appear detached, and they often state their opinions frankly. Once they choose a husband or wife, they prefer to stay with that person rather than changing. Five Soils have the ability to create their livelihood out of things they like to do.

Typical Occupations: Politician, government official,

educator, clergyman, thinker, philosopher, revolutionary, critic, manager, judge, warden, army officer, actor, doctor, real estate broker, financier, funeral director, auctioneer.

• **6 White Metal** – Both metal years produce people with very inwardly directed, self-disciplined characters. Strength, self-control, concern with ethical or orderly behavior and a keen, analytical sense of logic are common traits. Between the two, number 6 Metal types are slightly more intellectual. They often have some difficulty with social relations, finding it difficult to turn the focus of their energy outward and freely adapt to others' views or situations. Number 6 Metal is a silvery white, shining color, representing a slightly more clever, intellectual tendency. Six Metal people are very strong-willed and tend to act on their beliefs. They are not very talkative and don't yield so easily to other people's opinions. They dislike defeat and have clear, well-defined preferences.

Six Metal people have strong leadership abilities. Although they appear to have a lot of pride, they are often insecure. They are skillful at rising to the higher levels of an organization but may be unhappy if they don't reach the very top. They often scold their juniors and subordinates and try to impose discipline on others. As a result, other people respect them but often keep their distance.

People born in 6 Metal years are honest and straightforward. They have strong creative abilities and sometimes take on too many projects. They are fascinated by machinery and equipment and are attracted by tournaments and war. Their thinking tends to be conservative and is often ruled by the emotions. Women born under this sign often have a direct way of speaking and acting. Six Metals are active in romance, but their passions tend to shift rapidly from warm to cool.

Typical Occupations: Politician, public servant, lawyer, educator, thinker, financier, trader in precious metals, investor, airplane or car mechanic, assessor, guard, grain dealer, securities trader, mining engineer, athlete.

• **7 Red Metal** – People born under this sign are generally the most practical, most materially well-versed among all the nine types. They are not as intellectual or clever as number 6 Metal types but tend to be very strong in everyday common sense and organizational powers.

Seven Metal people have bright and active natures. They are fashion-conscious and dress stylishly. They are good at human relations and often act as peacemakers or mediators in group conflicts. They sometimes have a bossy character. They are attracted to luxurious surroundings and like to dine out. Being able to speak well is often the key to success for persons with this number. Their love relationships are guided by common sense. Although members of the opposite sex find them attractive, 7 Metals are often choosy about their partners. They excel at work and are good at handling money. Seven Metal people are often noticed by seniors and are promoted to positions of importance.

Typical Occupations: Accountant, trader, administrator, professor, lecturer, lawyer, secretary, city planner, martial arts expert, revolutionary, artist, dentist, entertainer, financier, hostess, salesperson, restaurant or nightclub manager, jewelry store manager.

8 White Soil – Number 8 is the most yang of the three soil types; this white is a shining, stark white like sand, rocky soil, or porcelain. These people are usually more serious, silent, deep thinkers, with a very refined, very intelligent character. Their opinions are carefully thought out and quite firm; they are so self-reliant that in the extreme, they may tend to become isolated or stubborn.

Eight Soil people have bright, optimistic natures. They are hard-working individualists who tend to be quiet and introspective. They have good memories and don't repeat the same mistakes twice. They approach new relationships with caution, but once friendship is established, the bonds are deep and long-lasting. Eight Soils frequently experience a crisis in middle age, but receive support from seniors or family members, and are able to recoup and again become successful. They use the lessons learned from failure to achieve success in later life. Eight Soils need good friends in order to achieve success.

Many 8 Soils are adventurers, and people born under this sign tend to change their residence often. Many 8 Soils receive an inheritance from their father or grandfather. Because they are gentle on the outside and strong on the inside, they are well liked. However, if they pursue material desires exclusively, people may dislike them. They are good planners and have a wealth of ideas. They have a clear sense of justice that can sometimes lead to conflict with established ideas. They are well-liked and respected by their colleagues. In marriage, they tend to stick with one partner and don't change their minds easily. Their relationships are usually steady, and not overly passionate or overly cool. If they pursue outside affairs, these are usually not serious.

Typical Occupations: Educator, lawyer, scientist, researcher, banker, financier, building manager, warehouse manager, policeman, guard, educator, revolutionary.

9 Purple Fire – This is the highest and most active level of energy within the cycle of nine. People born during this year are very active, outgoing, happy sociable types, usually very good at putting energy into and accomplishing goals that may have been formulated by others; and they are usually very adept at dealing with the public. The opposite of 1 White Water, who often appear to have no particular opinion, 9 Purple Fire people seem to have a very clear opinion on just about any topic. These views may be very poorly thought out or superficial, however; and these people easily tend to be impulsive and to act without thinking deeply.

Nine Fires have strong appetites for knowledge, and quick, sharp minds. They often find it hard to make friends with people whose opinions differ from theirs. They act positively to accomplish their objectives, but sometimes lack kindness. Nine Fires tend to be overconfident and often pay too much attention to details. They are sometimes

41

quick to point out other people's defects, but do not accept criticism easily.

Nine Fires are especially good at public relations. Some people born under this sign have liberal attitudes toward sex, while others have the opposite tendency. Nine Fire women often marry men who are more intellectual and socially established. After marriage, 9 Fires often become self- centered in their family relationships. They have difficulty working as a part of a team and are more successful when pursuing their goals independently. They are often financially successful.

Typical Occupations: Politician, thinker, writer, scholar, journalist, artist, craftsman, photographer, advertising executive, actor, accountant, judge, fashion model, beautician, fashion designer, television or radio announcer, doctor, teacher.

Primary and Secondary Nature

For general use, I recommend that you consider the Nine Star birth year as a person's primary character, or deep, long-term overall direction, and the season of birth as the secondary, or more outward, superficial character. For example, a person born during the autumn of a tree year will tend to appear very orderly, disciplined, and practical on the surface and in her expression, as a manifestation of the metal nature of her birth season. Using a larger view, however, you can see that her life is actually more concerned with more emotional, poetic, or non-conforming activities. She may, for example, be an avant-garde poet who types her manuscripts very neatly and has trouble getting published. Bear in mind that this secondary, seasonal influence is more material, more tangible; therefore, not only the season but also the particular location and climate of birth has a bearing here. Also, the seasons of the Northern and Southern hemisphere are opposite, while the Nine Star year qualities are global.

Before you go on reading, take a few minutes and make a list of your family members, close friends, and associates;

write down the season and year of birth for each, and figure out primary and secondary character types. Then check this against their actual personalities, ways of expression, and types of activities they enjoy, seeing how well you can correlate this information to the traits we have just studied.

As you continually check people's birthdates and explore these primary and secondary natures, you will gradually find that all people of one particular type have an underlying very similar nature; while they may not physically look alike, the way they behave, the way they express themselves, often even their facial expressions, all look strikingly similar.

A third influence comes from the particular Nine Star Ki nature of your month of birth. As we saw above, each month has a characteristic energy that corresponds to one of the nine numbers. In *Figure 12*, we present the Nine Star correlations with the months from 1990 to 2000. You can use this chart to calculate backward and determine the Nine Star Ki character of your month of birth. Please remember, however, that the energy of each month does not begin on the first calendar day of that month. Refer to *Figure 10* for the dates when the energy of each month changes. If you were born earlier in the month, consider your energy nature to be that of the previous month.

The influence of the monthly number is particularly strong during childhood and is more important than the year of birth in determining the personality type. At age eighteen, the year of birth takes over as the primary influence affecting character and destiny. Therefore, when determining the primary Nine Star Ki personality type in children under eighteen, use the month of birth. In adults, the month of birth continues to influence the personality, especially the emotions and outward expression.

Oriental Astrology and Relationships

The basic principle guiding personal relationships is simply the attraction of opposites, or polarity. Suppose you were born in December and your friend was born in April.

	1990	1991	1992	1993	1994	1995	1996	1997	1998	1999	2000
January	9	6	3	9	6	3	9	6	3	9	6
February	8	5	2	8	5	2	8	5	2	8	5
March	7	4	1	7	4	1	7	4	1	7	4
April	6	3	9	6	3	9	6	3	9	6	3
May	5	2	8	5	2	8	5	2	8	5	2
June	4	1	7	4	1	7	4	1	7	4	1
July	3	9	6	3	9	6	3	9	6	3	9
August	2	8	5	2	8	5	2	8	5	2	8
September	1	7	4	1	7	4	1	7	4	1	7
October	9	6	3	9	6	3	9	6	3	9	6
November	8	5	2	8	5	2	8	5	2	8	5
December	7	4	1	7	4	1	7	4	1	7	4

Figure 12:   Nine Star Months from 1990–2000

Passing the earlier part of your gestation period during the hotter season while your mother was consuming more yin foods, you would be generally more yin, while your friend would be generally more yang. Since yang is attracted to yin and vice versa, this would constitutionally tend to make you a very dynamic, well-polarized couple.

Several years ago, a student who learned this realized that he was born only one month apart from his wife. He immediately divorced her and proposed to a woman who-was born 182 days away from him, at the absolute opposite time of year. He thought that this polarity would make for a happy marriage. After living together for two months, they separated.

Why didn't this work? Very simply, that student was considering only time of year as the deciding factor; but there are many other factors to consider. Yes, 180-day opposition on the calendar is ideal for strong polarity, but that may be mediated by, for example, the place of birth. Suppose the yin-born person was born in Canada, while the more yang-born person was born in Florida. This would give a yang aspect to the yin person, and a more yin aspect to the yang person. For strong polarity, the place of birth should also preferably be strongly polarized.

Next, we should also check the lunar calendar: when the moon is bright and full, atmospheric conditions are very yang, while a dark new moon is opposite. People born during these two times may not be complete opposites, but there may be enough opposition to maintain dynamic polarity in this relationship. Being born and raised in the city or in the country are very different conditions and create strong polarity, as does being born on the plains or in the mountains, or inland or by the shore. Complementarity also arises from being born in two different countries, or even two different hemispheres; being born into a poor, hardworking family who of necessity eat fairly simply, or being born into a rich family; or growing up in a family of artists or a family of businessmen.

All of these factors and many others all play an integral

part in making up the nature of each individual, and less obvious factors may often be hidden by other more obvious influences; also, various combinations may become harmonious in ways that are not apparent on the surface. There is a great danger in seeing only a few conceptual factors. In fact, the best way to choose a partner is to use your intuition. At the first glimpse, you should already know whether or not you and that person will make a good combination.

However, our intuition is not always working so well. So, bearing in mind the infinite multiplicity of environmental factors determining one's individual constitution and character, let's study the use of astrology in relationships.

Month of Birth

First, let's consider what time of year you were born. After conception you spent about nine months in utero; during that time, the nine constellations of the Zodiac that correspond to those nine months were contributing their influence to the nine corresponding meridians and internal organs, one by one. This means that three months and their corresponding three constellations were skipped, not directly influencing you until your first three months of life. Therefore, the three organs and meridians that correspond to those three skipped months were to some degree lacking in your prenatal development, and these are constitutionally weaker organs. To determine which are your constitutionally weaker organs, refer to *Figure 13*. Begin at your birthday and count forward three months (these were the three months prior to your conception).

Depending on when the two of you were born, you may have one or several shared weaknesses, or you may have completely opposite, complementary weaknesses.

• **Born At Opposite Seasons (6 Months Apart)** – In terms of your meridians, you each have strengths where the other has weakness; and this generates a strong attrac-

Zodiac	Organs or Functions
Aquarius	Liver, lungs, large intestine
Pisces	Lung, large intestine, stomach
Aires	Large intestine, stomach, spleen
Taurus	Stomach, spleen, heart
Gemini	Spleen, heart, small intestine
Cancer	Heart, small intestine, bladder
Leo	Small intestine, bladder, kidney
Virgo	Bladder, kidney, heart governor*
Libra	Kidney, heart governor, triple heater*
Scorpio	Heart governor, triple heater, gall bladder
Sagitarrius	Triple heater, gall bladder, liver
Capricorn	Gall bladder, liver, lung

Figure 13: Constitutionally Weaker Organs

tion. Your sexual life is bound to be strong and active, provided you are both in good health, and you will tend to be drawn closer and closer together as your marriage goes on. This strong attraction often results in a very close bond, providing a deep and satisfying relationship even in old age after sexual activity ceases.

---

*The heart governor is not a specific organ but represents the body functions involved in the circulation of blood and body fluids. Similarly, the triple heater corresponds to the bodywide functions of metabolism and the generation of heat and caloric energy.

• **Born One Season (3 Months) Apart** – Again, you have no organ or meridian weaknesses in common, but in this case there is not as much constitutional attraction. This tends to be a marriage which may lack some charm or romance, but is full of variety, ups and downs. You may often have different opinions and contradictory points of view and need to develop tolerance and patience.

• **Born in Overlapping Seasons (2 Months Apart)** – You have several constitutional weaknesses in common, though not all, and because of this, you tend to understand each other very easily, and naturally tend to help each other. At the same time, your marriage tends to be a little one-sided, and this may become a disadvantage; for example, you may both tend to develop the same kinds of sicknesses.

• **Born the Same Month** – You share very similar organ strengths and weaknesses, although of course there will be some differences according to the diets of your parents and other prenatal influences. This creates a strong attraction of a sort, in that you almost automatically relate very well to each other, and if the geography of birth and family backgrounds are similar, you tend to develop an almost brother-sister type of friendship. However, it is very easy for one of you to be lured away by a third person born at the opposite time of year. In order to stay together, you need to have or develop the same dreams and same goals and to go out into society and actively pursue those goals.

Year of Birth

Suppose you were born during a number 9 year. If you get together with another 9 Fire person, the two of you can easily relate to each other. You both regard life in a similar way and react to events in a similar way. If the two of you marry, although the polarity between you is not so strong in terms of your Nine Star type, you are bound to communicate very well and have a good basis for developing together.

If you get together with a person born during a 2 Soil, 5 Soil, or 8 Soil year, what kind of relationship can you expect? You are a very energetic and active, friendly, sociable person, while the Soil person is more serious, thoughtful, and stable. Whatever initiatives that person takes, you will tend to lend your energies to helping accomplish that goal. In terms of the five transformations, your energy supports or nourishes that gathering, harmonizing type of energy.

In the ancient world, this type of marriage was considered ideal: one person's sign supports and strengthens the other person's. Strictly speaking, they usually recommended that the wife's sign be the first, supporting sign, so that the wife would support and further the energy of the husband; in other terms, this is the "parent-child" relationship, with the wife being "parent" and the husband being "child." In modern society, this might be reversed: you may prefer to have the husband's energy supporting and nurturing the wife's. But in either case, this is a very ideal, harmonious type of polarity between two people.

Nine Star Ki in Love and Relationships

Each of the nine character types has a different approach to love and relationships. Below we present these general tendencies according to the Nine Star Ki birth year, showing the positive and negative aspect of each sign.

• **1 Water** – People born under this sign take an active interest in romance and sometimes have many love affairs. However, their easy-going natures make it difficult for them to know where where to draw the line and so they sometimes wind up in interesting situations.

• **2 Soil** – People born in 2 Soil years are very trustworthy and serious when it comes to romance. Two Soil men are sometimes playboys. Men and women born during these years may display too much kindness. Two Soil women have a tendency to interfere in other people's affairs and may become isolated.

• **3 Tree** – From a young age, 3 Tree people have a strong interest in the opposite sex. Their destiny is to be active and happy in this domain. However, they are often overly possessive and experience jealousy. Three Trees need to work on their romantic and emotional natures.

• **4 Tree** – People born in these years are strongly attracted to love and romance and often meet partners unexpectedly. Four Tree women sometimes attract older men who act as protectors. Both men and women sometimes have trouble making decisions and often miss good opportunities. Four Tree women who divorce usually remarry.

• **5 Soil** – Soil 5 people are often involved in unusual situations. There may be a big age difference between the 5 Soil and his or her partner, or the number 5 person may get involved in a love triangle. They have a strongly possessive nature and are usually dedicated partners. They often shift back and forth between passion and coolness.

• **6 Metal** – Although 6 Metals may appear disinterested in romance, they are strongly possessive of their partners. Six Metal men are sometimes intimidated by their wives, while women of this sign often have professional interests that detract from their romantic lives. 6 Metals often need to cultivate a stronger emotional or romantic nature.

• **7 Metal** – People born under this sign are destined to have a rich emotional life. Seven Metal women often posses native sex appeal. For many 7 Metals, love and romance are their number one priority. However, they sometimes ignore the practical side of relationships and may experience difficulty as a result.

• **8 Soil** – These realistic types are not overly passionate or romantic. They are strongly independent and are often not attracted to deep romantic involvements. Many 8 Soil women remain single. Both men and women are reserved when it comes to expressing their emotions.

• **9 Fire** – People born in 9 Fire years tend to base their judgments on external appearances. They have strong preferences and tend to be liked by many people. They often receive romantic invitations, but may get into trouble if they are not careful.

Now suppose your sign is 9 Fire and you get together with a 6 Metal or 7 Metal person, who naturally tends to be very well organized. That person's energy is very inward, steady, and practical. Since you are very outgoing, very impulsive, and frequently changing your mind, you tend to override and frustrate the other person. Every time he tries to get things clear and orderly, you will come along with another brainstorm; he will always be trying to develop a practical, step-by-step plan, and you will want to pull him out of the house to go somewhere. Or if he suggests going out to hear classical music, you may insist on going to a late-night disco and he will probably forget about Mozart and go along with you. If this happens occasionally, it is not such a problem. But in this case, it tends to become a repeating pattern and can lead to underlying frustration. In other words, your energies are contradictory, following the *Ko* or control cycle described in the section on the five transformations, and it will be very difficult to stay together, to have the same friends, eat the same food, or follow the same dream.

Or, suppose you marry a 1 Water person. You are always expressing very headstrong opinions and strong ideas, but his easy-going, naturally adaptable character will constantly tend to put out your flames! In the first case, you were the controlling or suppressing agent; in this case, water energy controls you, and you are the frustrated party.

Traditionally, this third type of relationship was not recommended, and from my experience, it is a very antagonistic, difficult type of marriage. Although I don't check up every case, I have given consultations to many, many

51

couples who were unhappy and wanted to divorce. Every time I do notice their years of birth and make the Nine Star correlations, it is this type of relation, by the *Ko Cycle*. Usually with this type of marriage, the two are constantly quarreling; each one think the other is bad. Actually neither one is a bad person, only the combination is not so good.

Three Types of Marriage

Now let's review these three types of marriage, looking at the front and back or advantages and disadvantages of each type.

• **Marriage of Harmony** (Both with the Same Sign) – *Front*: you can easily understand each other and communicate very well, experiencing different situations in a very similar way, almost like brother and sister or classmates. This tends to make a very peaceful, happy marriage. *Back*: this peacefulness can also become rather dull. Since your home life is so harmonious, you cannot easily develop yourselves unless you actively go out and seek challenges in the outside world. If you don't do this, then it is very easy for a) your marriage to become more and more boring, and gradually dissolve, or b) one of you to suddenly become strongly attracted to a third person who is your complete opposite. While you may not understand that person as well as your spouse, he or she may give you a more exciting, romantic feeling.

• **Polarized or Supporting Marriage** (Two Consecutive Signs: Tree and Fire, Fire and Soil, Soil and Metal, Metal and Water, Water and Tree) – *Front:* in this case, there is enough polarity between you to make your lives together interesting and for each of you to develop and challenge the other to some degree. At the same time, since the close relationship of leading and supporting exists, one of you can easily go out into society and be active, and you can easily extend your marriage outward. *Back:* the downside of this marriage is not so large, but you may at some point be-

Sign	Supports	Is Supported By	Overrides	Is Overriden By
9 Fire	2, 5, 8 Soil	3, 4 Tree	6, 7 Metal	1 Water
8 Soil	6, 7 Metal	9 Fire; 2, 5 Soi	1 Water	3, 4 Tree
7 Metal	1 Water	2, 5, 8 Soil; 6 Metal	3, 4 Tree	9 Fire
6 Metal	1 Water; 7 Metal	2, 5, 8 Soil	3, 4 Tree	9 Fire
5 Soil	6,7 Metal	9 Fire; 2 Soil	1 Water	3, 4 Tree
4 Tree	9 Fire	1 Water; 3 Tree	2, 5, 8 Soil	6, 7 Metal
3 Tree	9 Fire; 4 Tree	1 Water	2, 5, 8 Soil	6, 7 Metal
2 Soil	6, 7 Metal; 5, 8 Soil	9 Fire	1 Water	3, 4 Tree
1 Water	3, 4 Tree	6, 7 Metal	9 Fire	2, 5, 8 Soil

Figure 14: Supporting and Overriding Relationships
Within the Nine Star Ki

gin to feel one-sided, and want the supporting person to take the lead more and the leading person to be more supportive.

• **Antagonistic Marriage** (Opposite Signs: Tree and Soil, Fire and Metal, Soil and Water, Metal and Tree, Water and Fire) – *Back:* (I have put the back first since it is more obvious): you cannot understand each other, communicate with each other, or agree with each other. You tend to contradict each other at every turn. *Front:* if you harmonize yourselves enough, can together work out a way of sharing and communicating, and can learn to overcome your differences, then your relationship can become tremendously strong. Without even going outside your house, there is enough challenge to really develop both of you. Learning to harmonize this marriage can teach you a great deal about life, and make you into a very flexible person. If you can go on to take on more outside challenges, your contributions to society can be unique and very valuable, though it may take many years before you can reach this point.

In addition to Nine Star Ki, you can also check your various relationships in terms of the *Twelve Shi*. If you are born during, let's say, a Tiger year, then you can marry someone else who is also a Tiger; naturally you will tend to have a very compatible, harmonious, or almost brother–sister relationship. If you marry someone at the opposite pole, in this case a Monkey, then your relationship will be much more antagonistic and exciting, as well as more difficult. Traditionally, the most ideal combinations for a harmonious marriage are 1) consecutive signs, which for a Tiger would be a Cow or Rabbit, and 2) triangle signs or signs that are four stages apart, which for a Tiger would be a Horse or Dog. Also if you are both the same sign, that can be a very happy marriage.

If your combination works well according to both of these systems, that is very auspicious: you will probably have a wonderful marriage. If you are very antagonistic according to one system, but combine well according to the other, then you can safely go ahead and marry, expecting there to be some difficulty of adjustment and some compromising needed.

Strengthening An Antagonistic Relationship

However, if your combination is constitutionally antagonistic according to both systems, the relationship could be difficult. Since neither astrological influence is bringing you together, what can you do? First, there may be some other, more obvious constitutional factor that helps your combination: since you are antagonistic astrologically, look to see if your birth month, geography of birth, family and ancestral occupations, or other background factors may be bringing you together. And don't forget that the attraction of the sexes is itself the most powerful polarity bringing you together; that is already sufficient to make any marriage possible. But in this third, most antagonistic case, there is a way to transcend the potential conflicts that may arise. Although you cannot change the inherent character you each created by the times of birth you chose, you can by your free will change the quality of that character through your food.

There are two important aspects of using your food to make your marriage stabilize: health and harmony. Health in this case, means this: although your two characters tend to conflict, if you are both in a very healthy, clean, calm and balanced physiological condition, eating very good food which has been prepared in a very clean, orderly manner according to the principles of yin and yang or the order of the universe, then neither of you will manifest that contradictory nature in too extreme a way. Most couples who have this kind of conflicting nature tend to eat more extreme foods, each choosing the particular extreme their nature favors. That extreme eating pulls them farther and farther apart. If you both eat more toward the center, it will be much easier to establish a harmonious center for your marriage. In this case, it is also particularly important to not overeat.

Harmony simply means: eat the same food. Naturally, because you are man and woman, there will be some slight differences in your eating preferences, and because of your individual natures there will be some differences. But to establish a better base for communication, it is especially important for you to eat together, eating generally the same food, as often as possible. Through your daily eating, you can grow together toward the same tendencies and same dream, though you will always still have somewhat different interpretations of that dream.

Interestingly enough, it was recently found that when two people live together, eat the same food, and exchange small volumes of their individual chemical makeup through kissing, touching each other and sex, the actual composition of DNA in each begins to gradually change, each taking on certain characteristics of the other. So no matter what your birth signs are, once you have chosen a certain partner for life, it is easily within your grasp to change yourselves enough to keep that commitment throughout your life.

Nine Star Ki and Health

Suppose two people have come to see you for advice, both on the same day and both with similar problems; let's say both are suffering from weak, over-worked kidneys. (They may have told you this, or you may have noticed it yourself by observing such familiar diagnostic features as dark circles under the eyes, a posturally tight lower back, or a rigid, exclusive, even fearful mood.) When they first come in, they both have written down their names, addresses, and dates of birth: one was born in the spring of 1945, and the other in the autumn of 1947. Both of them appear somewhat dark and serious, and even a little stubborn.

Should you give them the same general advice? And if not, how should your approach differ for each? Please think this question over carefully before reading on: what do these birth dates tell you about that condition in each?

You have probably already studied many different techniques for seeing a person's condition and know a variety of approaches to Oriental diagnosis, but never forget that everyone is different: you always need to evaluate a person's condition in terms of how it relates to that person's own unique constitution, including the season and year of birth.

In the case above, although the two people's sicknesses may appear quite similar, the first person has probably abused his health more strenuously, and perhaps for a longer period of time, than the second person; and your advice should be adjusted accordingly. For example, the first person may need much more detailed advice, and you may want to suggest that he come back to see you several times so you can check on his progress and further adjust your recommendations. The second person will probably follow your advice more easily, and heal himself more quickly, probably needing no further visits. How can you tell this?

The first person was born in 1945, a 1 Water year; further, he was born in the spring. That gives him the constitutional tendency to be strong in which organs? His water nature organs, the kidneys, bladder, adrenals, and sex organs represent the year of his birth, and their energy should naturally be strong. This also gives his personality a basic, constitutional tendency to be flexible, easy-going, and adaptable. According to his season of birth, the spring-time, you would also expect his outward appearance of immediate character to be bright, outgoing, very light, and perhaps a little spontaneous, like the energy of spring.

Instead, the person standing before you is dark and serious, with a very heavy, somber mood. Rather than being flexible, he appears stubborn and unbending. In other words, he has abused his physical health to the point where his very constitutional character has been suppressed. For this to have happened, that abuse would have had either to be very pronounced, to be maintained over a long time, or both. The second person tends by birth to be a little more serious, due to his autumn birth, so this should be cause for no great concern. Further, as he was born in an 8 Soil year, his spleen, stomach, and pancreas are the organs receiving the strongest constitutional energy. These soil nature organs are antagonistic to the water organs, so it should come as no surprise that he may chronically have some trouble or weakness in his kidneys. By recommending some slight adjustments to his diet, and perhaps offering a few additional suggestions on how to strengthen his kidneys, such as simple exercises or an external treatment like ginger compress, you will probably be giving that person all he needs to take care of the problem.

As soon as you learn a person's date of birth, even if you have not even seen the person himself, you can already assemble a fairly detailed picture of his or her general character, health tendencies, and even dietary preferences. If, after forming such a picture, you meet the person and discover that your image is totally wrong, this means a) the person has substantially abused his or her health, burying the true self within a morass of excess, or b) you have the wrong dates. While it may take a little practice to accurately see the correlations between a person's appearance and health and his birth date, the correspondence is always there; the method is accurate, only your interpretation and application of it may lead you to inaccurate conclusions. The more you practice, the more precise you will become. As a basis for your own continuing study, let's look at some basic general correlations.

• **Constitutionally Strong Organs** – The energy of the organs that correspond to your Nine Star Ki year of birth tend to have stronger functions than your other organs. These are determined by the energy transformations (within the five transformations) that correspond to your year of birth, and these correspondences are presented in *Figure 15*.

• **Constitutionally Weaker Organs** – Those organs that correspond to the two transformations opposite to your year of birth tend to have slightly weaker or more vulnerable functioning. For example, a person born in 1952 (a 3 Tree year) would tend to have a strong liver and gall bladder, but his or her spleen, stomach, pancreas, lungs and large intestine would be slightly more susceptible to weakness.

• **Constitutional Food Preferences** – Most people are instinctively drawn to foods that correspond to those transformations opposite to their own sign. According to this principle, the person in the example (tree nature) would be drawn to foods of either soil or metal nature, such as sweets or spicy tastes.

• **Effects of Food Preferences** – Indulging in those particular food preferences to a moderate degree and with good quality foods will tend to strengthen the corresponding constitutionally weaker organs. In the above example, a small volume of foods like sweet hard squash or well-cooked carrots, and a mild spicy taste like grated daikon,

Birth Year	Energy	Strong Organs	Weaker Organs	Food Preferences	Food Effects
3 & 4	Tree	Liver/gall bladder (tree Eeergy)	Spleen, pancreas/ stomach (soil); lungs/large intestine (metal)	Sweet (soil) and spicy (metal) foods	Strengthening of weaker organs; weakening of strong organs— kidney/bladder (water) and liver/gall bladder (tree)
9	Fire	Heart/small intestine (fire Eeergy)	Lungs/large intestine (metal); kidney/bladder (water)	Spicy (metal) and salty (water) foods	Strengthening of weaker organs; weakening of strong organs— liver/gall bladder (tree) and heart/small intestine (fire)
2, 5, & 8	Soil	Spleen, pancreas/ stomach (soil energy)	Kidney/bladder (water); liver/gall bladder (tree)	Salty (water) and sour (tree) foods	Strengthening of weaker organs; weakening of strong organs— heart/small intestine (fire) and spleen, pancreas/stomach (soil)
6 & 7	Metal	Lungs/large intestine (metal energy)	Liver/gall bladder (tree); heart/small intestine (fire)	Sour (tree) and bitter (fire) foods	Strengthening of weaker organs; weakening of strong organs— spleen, pancreas/stomach (soil) and lungs/large intestine (metal)
1	Water	Kidney/bladder (water energy)	Heart/small intestine (fire); spleen, pancreas/ stomach (soil)	Bitter (fire) and sweet (soil) foods	Strengthening of weaker organs; weakening of strong organs— lungs/large intestine (metal) and kidney/bladder (water)

Fig. 15: Organ Strengths and Weaknesses and Food Preferences and Effects

chopped raw scallions, or mustard greens will help stimulate and strengthen this person's spleen, stomach, pancreas, lungs, and large intestine.

However, every special treatment has both an advantage and a disadvantage. Overindulging in those types of foods or eating a poor or extreme quality of those foods will, according to the *Ko Cycle* (antagonistic relation) begin to weaken the opposite pairs of organs, in this case, the kidneys and bladder (water), and the liver and gall bladder (tree). As a result, most people tend to follow a pattern of food preferences that damages or weakens the organs corresponding to their own sign and the previous sign, or their own transformation and its "parent."

Simply speaking, this is an example of the principle that we always tend to abuse our greatest strengths. Therefore, the organs, meridians, thought patterns, emotions, types of behavior, and overall characteristics that are associated with a person's year of birth are precisely those that will most easily tend to become the sickest or weakest, and these tendencies are summarized in the table in *Figure 15*.

Diagnosis by Five Transformations

Let us briefly summarize some of the appearances these disorders or energy imbalances take.

• **Postural Manifestations** – You can easily see general troubles in certain pairs of organs by looking for tightness in certain areas of the back. You can do this by observing the person's posture or by directly pressing on those areas. *Figure 16* shows the correlation of each area to the particular transformation and organ-pair.

• **Psychological Manifestations** – There are also a variety of emotions, mental states, and types of expression that indicate trouble in these five areas. Referring to figure 17, please try to understand why each symptom appears when the associated organs are troubled, in terms of the type of energy that is being blocked or frustrated. Tree nature ener-

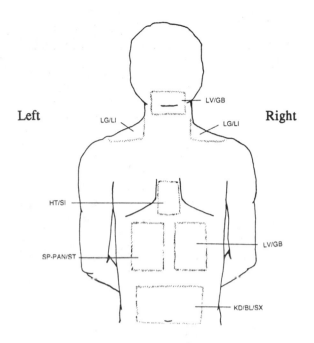

Figure 16: Diagnosis of Internal Organs by Observing Tightness in Regions of the Back

gy, for example, is rising, expanding, very light and spring-like energy. When this is blocked by eating overly yang food or by other factors, that expanding energy cannot pass smoothly through the liver and gall bladder. As a result, energy accumulates and finally bursts out in irregular, overactive, at times even violent spurts. Emotionally, we interpret this as anger or as shouting. You can understand all these symptoms by applying the same kind of reasoning and imagination.

• **Time of Day or Year** – If certain symptoms, whether physical or psychological, appear consistently at certain times of the day or during certain seasons, you can also explore the correlation with that particular transformation. Recurrent problems in the morning or in the spring, for example, may indicate a basic problem in the liver/gall bladder.

61

	TREE	FIRE	SOIL	METAL	WATER
Energy type	Ascending energy	Active, expanded energy	Descending, gathering energy	Dense, fully materialized energy	Dissolving, floating energy
Mental/ Psychological symptoms	Anger, com-plaining, abusive, argumentative, violent	Excitable, nervous, over-emotional, hysterical, sentimental	Doubt, suspicion, cynicism, critical, cold	Attatchment, stubborn, depression	Fear, insecurity, protective, exclusive, defensive
Active symptoms	Shout, argue	Talkative, nervous laughter	Incessant whistling, singing, humming	Sighing, crying	Whimpering, groaning
Time of vulnerability	Spring/morning	Summer/noon	Late summer/ afternoon	Autumn/evening	Winter/night
Organs affected	Liver/gall bladder	Heart/small intestine, heart governor/triple heater	Spleen-pancreas/ stomach	Lung/large intestine	Kidney/bladder, adrenals/sex organs
Overriding nature	Metal	Water	Tree	Fire	Soil

Figure 17: Psychological Symptoms of Organ Troubles by the Five Transformations

As you already know, the organs that correspond to your Nine Star Ki year of birth tend to be particularly sensitive to excess; however, anybody can overtax and eventually weaken any of their organs, and it is helpful to know the various contributing causes in each case. Although diet is the most important, primary cause of organic disorders, mental, psychological, and emotional factors also play a role. Let us look at how these can effect our health.

Emotional Imbalances In Childhood

• **Tree Nature** – The rising, poetic nature of tree energy is weakened by repeated suppression: if a child receives no encouragement or emotional support, no appreciation or inspiration, or is prevented repeatedly from exploring his or her initiatives and curiosities, chronic trouble in the liver and gall bladder and a tendency toward anger may develop.

• **Fire Nature** – The highly energetic quality of fire nature is weakened by repeated indulgence: if a child is spoiled, over-indulged, never given strong guidance or discipline, or if the parents are overly sentimental, the tendency to act without thinking will become overly developed. Chronic trouble in the heart and small intestine and a tendency toward over-excited, hysterical behavior may develop.

• **Soil Nature** – The stabilized, balanced quality of soil nature is weakened by a human environment that is chronically unreliable, undependable, irresponsible, or hypocritical. The child will tend to develop spleen, pancreatic, and stomach problems and a general attitude of cynicism, doubt, or aimlessness.

• **Metal Nature** – The yang, firm, confident quality of metal nature is weakened by loneliness and a human environment lacking in warmth, sympathy, or compassion.

This child will tend to become depressed or melancholy and to develop trouble in the lungs and large intestine.

• **Water Nature** – The flexible, adaptable features of water nature are weakened by an over-protective human environment, by parents or parent figures who repeatedly instill fear, excessive caution, or exclusivity by overly strong criticism, warning, or frightening the child or by excessive criticism of others. This child will tend to become chronically fearful and exclusive, with the tendency toward kidney and bladder problems, as well as possible sexual weakness or dysfunction.

Restoring Psychological Balance

On a more immediate basis, a person will tend to react to an overly stressful situation with the response that overrides his or her own nature: for example, a normally flexible, adaptable 1 Water person, who may have developed a tendency toward timidity and self-protection, will tend when suddenly confronted with an extremely frightening situation to respond by becoming extremely cynical. A normally excitable, outgoing and happy 9 Fire person may under stress suddenly become paralyzed with fear, and so on.

When confronted with any of the above problems, it may at times be appropriate to give a person practical advice on his or her way of life and mental orientation, to help balance these extreme traits and restore a more orderly mental state. These recommendations may be applied to people of the corresponding Nine Star Ki type, or to other people who have developed troubles related to those specific transformations and organs.

• **Tree Nature** – This person needs to make his or her life more orderly and peaceful; in extreme cases, the person may need to go to the mountains, a forest area, a monastery, or some other secluded, peaceful place, to be within quiet surroundings and reflect in solitude.

• **Fire Nature** – This person needs more responsibility and discipline; he should carefully regulate his life, organizing his activities with a clearly defined schedule and even a self-evaluating and grading system, to make himself more punctual and yang. Clear plans for the future should also be worked out.

• **Soil Nature** – This person tends to think too much, and needs to find very practical pursuits. Farming, gardening, or dealing with nature are especially helpful.

• **Metal Nature** – This person needs warmth, inspiration, compassion, loving care, and sympathy. She needs to create a human environment for herself that encourages and supports her.

• **Water Nature** – This person needs to become more open and socially active, even worldly; he may achieve this by having contact with a wide range of people, situations and ideas, traveling, generally enlarging his social life, or even to some degree by reading a wide variety of books depicting a range of life situations, such as biographies or historical novels.

Of course, such advice is not necessary in every case; when the problems involved are not too severe or overly developed, it is often enough to simply encourage certain of the person's stronger points. Examples of these points, according to the person's birth sign, are as follows:

• **Tree Nature** – Idealism, imagination, artistic ability, creativity, romantic qualities; this person may have religious or spiritual leanings, which should be encouraged.

• **Fire Nature:** – Kindness, generosity, open-heartedness, sociability, compassion.

• **Soil Nature** – Thoughtfulness, inventiveness, creative thinking.

	TREE	FIRE	SOIL	METAL	WATER
Foods that correlate (supporting energy)	barley, wheat, oats	corn	millet	rice	buckwheat, azuki beans
	rapidly growing, young greens, sprouts	large leafy greens	round vegetables	root vegetables	compact, spikey greens, seaweeds
	sour tast	bitter taste	sweet taste	pungent tast	salty taste
Foods that harm (counteracting energy)	Metal nature	Water nature	Tree nature	Fire nauure	Soil nature
	oil, fat, heavy foods, sweets, spices, alcohol	animal food, excess salt, spices, excess liquid, fruit	dairy food, refined flour, excess sweets, greasy food	fruit, sugar, excess liquid, baked flour products, fat & oil	excess liquid, excess salt, raw food, sweets, over-cooked (baked) foods, stimulants, cold food or drink

Figure 18: Positive and Negative Effects of Different Foods

• **Metal Nature** – Disciplined self-development, organizational ability, practicality.

• **Water Nature** – Adaptability, flexibility, social tact, and diplomacy (ability to see both sides of a disagreement).

Bear in mind that these mental symptoms may not always be readily apparent when you talk to a person; also it is not necessary to use the more psychological types of treatment or advice given above in every case. Diet, however, is the one universal underlying cause of problems, and the one universal way of restoring balance. Listed in *Figure 18* are the five transformations together with their associated foods, examples of foods that cause imbalance or stagnation in each, and types of foods that can help restore a healthy condition in each. As an example, if you see a person that is clearly suffering from liver/gall bladder troubles, you can suspect that he has eaten some overly yang, heavy or fatty foods, and can suggest that he cook barley together with brown rice as his staple grain for a while, make sure to include green leafy vegetables such as scallions or dandelion greens in his diet, and in general emphasize a lighter, fresher style of cooking until the problem begins to diminish. In some cases a light sour taste can help, such as umeboshi, rice vinegar, lemon juice, or sauerkraut. Sometimes, however, excessive poor-quality sour foods have been contributing to the problem, such as citrus drinks or commercial vinegar. When and how to use these five special tastes is a matter of practice and experience.

The Two Nine Star Ki Groups

We can also simplify this approach by categorizing all nine types into two general groups, one more yin group and one more yang group. Grouping together 6 Metal, 7 Metal, the two more yang Soils 5 and 8, and 1 Water gives us a category of more descending, yang types of energy. Two Soil, 3 and 4 Tree, and 9 Fire are all relatively more ascending, expanding, yin energy types. If you carefully observe many people of all different signs, you will find that these two groups exhibit many complementary patterns.

For example, those of the more yang, stabilized group are generally more comfortable in colder seasons or climates, since these conditions are more similar to their own nature. If these people travel to a hotter climate they often feel uncomfortable. People of the more yin group (2, 3, 4, 9) are more comfortable within a hotter climate, and tend to be less comfortable in the cold. During the full moon, 2, 3, 4, or 9 people function more comfortably. People in the more yang group tend to feel more uncomfortable during a full moon. During a new moon the opposite is true.

Likewise, above and beyond the individual food preferences discussed earlier, the people of the more yin group tend as a whole to prefer more yin foods, such as fruit, salad, liquid, and sweets and to prefer vegetable food over animal food. The yang group tend to prefer animal food, salty foods, hearty cooking, baked dishes, and other yang foods.

In general, when the energy of the earth's atmosphere is at a higher, active level, during a 2, 3, 4, or 9 year, month or day, the more yin group are more comfortable and active; during the years, months or days of a lower, more contracted and inactive energy level (1,5,6,7 or 8) those of the more yang group are more active and happy.

When you are helping someone to restore their own natural healthy condition, you can use more side dishes of land vegetables for those people of the more yin group, and more side dishes of sea vegetables for those of the more yang group; the yin group people may take slightly more liquid, while the yang group people may need slightly drier food and a little more cooking.

These are only general suggestions for your own continuing study; there are actually an infinite number of ways in which you can apply Nine Star Ki in your approach to different conditions. Beginning with the above as guidelines, see what kind of correlations you can draw while observing several hundred people. Gradually you can add your own conclusions and develop a highly refined understanding of Oriental astrology and the human condition.

Part II

Nine Star Ki and Human Destiny

The Universal Table ("Magic Square")

Thousands of years ago, before the world was divided into separate territorial kingdoms, ancient macrobiotic people had developed a highly refined cosmology that was well known throughout the world. Nine Star Ki is one aspect of this cosmology; another was the development of mandalas, or graphic/diagrammatic expressions of the order of the universe. These mandalas were used to create maps of the heavens, charts of meridians, agricultural calendars and many, many other practical applications. Actually, the development of mandalas is closely related to Nine Star Ki: the basic universal table (shown in *Figure 19*), upon which all the more complex tables and mandalas were based, is in fact a graphic illustration of the earth's atmospheric ki flow according to these nine stages, as we will see a little later on.

This simple table, known today to school children in the Orient as the "magic square," appears very simple. Upon closer study, however, it actually contains many, many lifetimes of study and experience; all of our macrobiotic understanding and cosmology can be expressed with this simple diagram. Before looking at some of its practical applications, let us take a brief look at some of the numerological implications of the universal table.

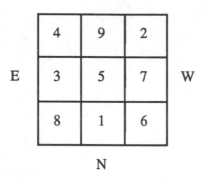

Figure 19: The Universal Table
(Magic Square)

The 81 Magic Square

In the basic universal table there are eight rows of three numbers each, including three horizontal rows, three vertical columns, and two diagonal rows. The "magic square's" most well-known feature is that any of these eight rows of three adds up to a total of 15 (which is also 3 times 5, the central number); for example, 6 + 5 + 4 = 15, 6 + 1 + 8 = 15, or 1 + 5 + 9 = 15. This shows the essential numerical integrity or unity of the basic table.

A second, more elaborate magic square can be produced from this simple table, having 81 places rather than 9 places (see *Figure 20*). By dividing these 81 numbers into 9 component squares of 9 numbers each, we can see how this larger array is generated from the original square: the first set of 9 numbers is arranged in the same sequence as in the basic table, each one occupying the "1 place" of its component square. Following the same procedure, the second set of 9 numbers, 10 through 18, is again arranged in the same sequence, now appearing in the "2 place" of each square. 19 through 27 are all placed in the "3 place" of each square, again in the same sequence, and so on.

Adding together the digits of any single number in any sub-square will produce the original single digit dominat-

31	76	13	36	81	18	29	74	11
22	40	58	27	45	63	20	38	56
67	**4**	49	72	**9**	54	65	**2**	47
30	75	12	32	77	14	34	79	16
21	39	57	23	41	59	25	43	61
66	**3**	48	68	**5**	50	70	**7**	52
35	80	17	28	73	10	33	78	15
26	44	62	19	37	55	24	42	60
71	**8**	53	64	**1**	46	69	**6**	51

E   W

N

Figure 20: The Eighty-One Magic Table

ing that sub-square. For example, in the lower right-hand or "6 square", 5 + 1 = 6, 6 + 9 = 15, which reduces to 6 (1 + 5), 6 + 0 = 6, 4 + 2 = 6, and so forth. In the bottom center square, all the numbers reduce to 1; and so on through all the component squares.

Taking the 81 numbers as a single magic square, any 9 numbers in any of the 20 straight rows (9 horizontal, 9 vertical, 2 diagonal) added together will produce 369; 369 divided by 9 yields 41, which is the central number of this larger square. Again, this shows the basic numerological integrity of this larger magic square.

The implications of this chart, which you may discover through deep study, are various and amazing. Almost all Oriental cosmology may be derived from this array of numbers, as can the basis of the ancient Chinese and Aztec calendars.

To calculate the length of the year, we begin with the number 369 which is the total of any straight row in *Figure 20*. In further calculation, the number 41 is not included, because it is constant. Between 1 and 100, we should subtract 1 as a token of the constant 41; between 100 and 200 another 41 occurs so we take out another 1; 1 is also removed for the numbers 200 to 300. However, we take out only 69/100 between 300 and 369 since only 69/100ths of 41 is represented there. Next we subtract 3.69 from 369 leaving a total of 365.31 days in the year. (The central number 41 and the digit 5 to which it reduces are significant in themselves.)

This brings us to the calendar reproduced in *Figure 21*. This chart is known in Japanese as *Kanagi-Guruma*, or "god manifested wagon"; the term "wagon" referring to the rotation of a wheel, or in other words, a recurring cycle. This chart was the origin of the *I Ching* and other Far Eastern cosmologies. The numbers within the circle are displayed in a definite order that is based on the array of numbers in the large square. Forty-one is the center, and the outer circle of numbers is the result of adding together and then reducing the corresponding numbers inside the circle. The reduced numbers also show the component square from which the inside digits have come. For example, 5 occurs whenever the central component square is indicated.

Each of the eighty numbers represents four or five days of the calendar year with the exception of the numbers that reduce to 5. These represent only one day. The four–day groups are spaced periodically throughout the year so that the total number of days is 365 and a fraction per year. The five-day period corresponds to a natural climatic cycle consisting of three days of yangization followed by two days of more yin weather.

Ancient people divided the year into twelve periods roughly corresponding to our modern twelve months, as well as the *Ju Ni Shi*, or twelve earthly influences. These are shown around the outside of the circle with their corresponding animal names. They also recognized eight pri-

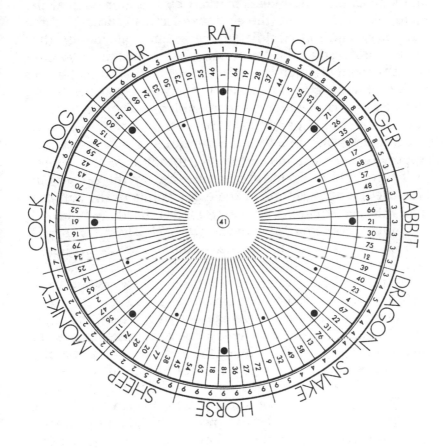

Figure 21: The Ancient Calendar (Kanagi-Garuma)*

* Note the following correspondences:

Rat	Rabbit	Horse	Cock
North	East	South	West
Winter	Spring	Summer	Autumn
Midnight	Morning	Midday	Evening

mary divisions of the year, marked by the four days at the middle of each season (the equinoxes and solstices) and the four days that fall equidistant between them; these latter were considered as the beginning of each season. For example, the ancient calendar located the beginning of spring not at the spring equinox, but halfway between the spring equinox and the winter solstice, which is February 4th or 5th. These special periods are marked by large black dots. The smaller black dots indicate the number 5 days that correspond to numbers in the central square.

These eight divisions are represented by the eight numbers occupying positions of the eight points of the compass in the larger square; starting from due north (winter solstice) and proceeding clockwise: 1, 71, 21, 31, 81, 11, 61, 51. The "1" digit in each represents initiation, or the beginning of a new period. These numbers and their corresponding times of year are shown in the table below. When these eight are added together they produce 328; adding this to 41, the number of the center, we again arrive at the constant of 369. 369, or "Mi-Ro-Ku" in Japanese, represents Miroku Bodhisattva, or the "Buddha of the Future" who is prophesied to descend to earth at the end of modern civilization and bring universal enlightenment to humanity.

There are actually countless practical and metaphysical applications of this ancient numerical table; and it is itself one of the few direct links we have with the ancient spiritual civilization existing prior to the catastrophes of 12,000 years ago, catastrophes that divided humanity into independent, self-interested territories. I hope you will make this table the subject of your study, and go far beyond the few aspects I am pointing out here.

Going back to the tables in *Figures 19 and 20*, can you guess why the directions of the compass are shown in the opposite order from the conventional way (upside-down and backwards)? This is still regarded as a great mystery and is the subject of much metaphysical debate; but the ancient thinkers who developed this table were very practical. They were drawing a map of the flow of earth's atmosphere and energy as a whole, particularly from the perspective of the celestial influence showering down on the earth from the constellations over the north pole. If you imagine yourself standing on the north pole, with these constellations above you and the earth at your feet, how would you draw the eight points of the compass?

If you study the Aztec calendar, you will find many similarities to the ancient Far Eastern calendar shown in *Figure 21*. At the center of the calendar is a big face symbolizing the central god or the number 41. There is another god in the south position who is like fire, and another god in the north who is like water. (The god in the south is the god of the sun.) The directions north, south, east, and west are also shown, and between them are four in-between points totalling 8 directions overall. These correspond to the numbers in *Figure 22* and indicate the equinoxes, solstices, and the beginning of the seasons. There are also eighty white numbers around the periphery, corresponding to the numbers in *Kanagi-Guruma*. Although at first glance these two representations appear different, they are essentially the same.

Number	Time of Year
1	Winter solstice
71	Beginning of spring
21	Spring equinox
31	Beginning of summer
81	Summer solstice
11	Beginning of autumn
61	Autumnal equinox
51	Beginning of winter

Fig. 22: Numbers and Correspondeng
Times of the Year

Individual Prediction

To begin interpreting this chart, first notice that the directions of the compass also relate to seasons, times of day, and types of energy. South, for example, represents summer, midday, and fire nature energy, as represented by number 9. As you can see, this arrangement of numbers also corresponds very closely to our usual circular diagram of the five transformations, with fire at the top, metal to the right and the descent, water at the bottom, and so forth. However, if you trace the progression numerically from 1 to 9 (or from 9 to 1), you get a very strange drawing shown in *Figure 23*.

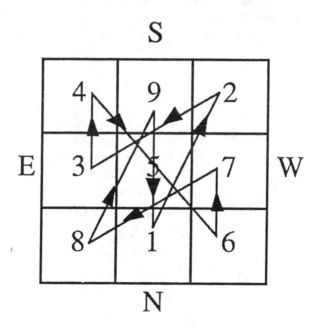

Figure 23: Movement of Atmospheric Energy Charted by Nine Star Ki

This tracing is very, very interesting. While it doesn't appear at first to make much sense in two dimensions, if you consider it as being three-dimensional, considering motion not only between north and south but also from higher above and closer down to the earth's surface, you can detect a very orderly, spiral pattern. This is the pattern of the atmosphere's motion, as it heats up and expands, cools off and contracts, shifting from north to south and back again, and shifting from east to west from the influence of the earth's rotation. This produces the earth's various wind currents, as well as a consistent motion of atmospheric energy through nine stages. (It is also interesting to note that this pattern creates two infinity signs superimposed on each other, one large and one small; this can be viewed as representing the motion of the infinitely large vibrational cosmos and of the infinitesimally small, material environment, coming together in our atmosphere.)

Every year, every month, and every day this map changes, shifting so that a new number comes into the center, generating a new sequence of directions. During a number 5 Yellow Soil year, such as 1995, the number 5 will occupy the center, producing the standard map. In 1996, this will shift to a new map with 4 in the center; 5 will move to the 6 place, 6 to the 7 place, and so on: every number proceeds along that atmospheric flow to the next place.

Therefore, we can assign a particular Nine Star Ki map to every day, month, and year. *Figure 24* shows the particular ki maps or "magic squares" for each year in the 1990s (keep in mind that the year begins on February 4), and *Figure 25* shows the ki maps for the months in 1991.

If you are a 9 Fire person (born during a 9 Fire year), 1991 will be "your" year, and July of '91 in particular is "your" month. Your number is in the center of that period's ki map; the earth's atmosphere is closely aligned to your own energy. During this time, everything naturally comes to you or is oriented towards you, in a sense, you become similar to a 5 Yellow Soil person in that you are now naturally the center of activity.

Because of this, it would not be wise for you to move

1993

4	9	8
2	7	3
6	5	1

1997

9	5	4
7	3	8
2	1	6

2001

5	1	9
3	8	4
7	6	2

1992

5	1	9
3	8	4
7	6	2

1996

1	6	5
8	4	9
3	2	7

2000

6	2	1
4	9	5
8	7	3

1991

6	2	1
4	9	5
8	7	3

1995

2	7	6
9	5	1
4	3	8

1999

7	3	2
5	1	6
9	8	4

1990

7	3	2
5	1	6
9	8	4

1994

3	8	7
1	6	2
5	4	9

1998

8	4	3
6	2	7
1	9	5

Figure 24: Ki Maps for Years in the 1990s

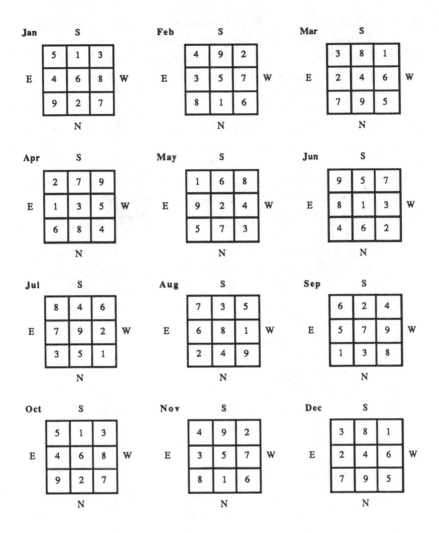

Figure 25: The Nine Star Ki Maps for the Months of 1991

around too much during 1991 (and especially during the month of July); too much movement, such as wide travels or intense activity, will tend to disturb this natural flow of energy and events coming toward you. Because this period's atmospheric condition matches very well with yours, it tends to support you; you are liable to feel comfortable and not have much trouble. In general, this is a good time for self-reflection, internal development, and preparation for the future. Whatever you are doing this year, and particularly in July, will tend to be successful and continue bearing fruit throughout the next nine years or nine months. By the same token, all your efforts of the past nine years (or months) tend to come to some conclusion during this period: if those pursuits have been well in harmony with your own true dreams and aspirations, the results at this time will tend to be very favorable; if you have been following any "blind alleys," pursuing activities or initiatives about which you do not really care or which are not truly in line with your own intuition, these things are liable to come to an end at this time.

In short, when your own number is in the center of the ki map for the current year, month, or even day, it is best to stabilize and stay to the center; this is a time of conclusion and renewal. During the other eight years, your number's position in the ki map changes around, following the double-figure eight path of atmospheric flow. Each position carries different influences and characteristics. To understand this principle, simply imagine that these eight directions of the compass represent eight times of day or year. During the summertime, or around noon, you naturally tend to be very active, outgoing, and talkative. You are moving at a fast pace and developing very quickly and dramatically. This corresponds to the south position, occupied in the standard table by the number 9 Fire.

Whenever your number appears in this position, you naturally tend to take on certain fire characteristics, to be active and busy, to lead a stronger public life, to become famous or travel and meet many people, and so on. If you want to engage in this kind of activity, then choosing a year or month when you are in that position will help you. However, if you are bent on spending most of your time studying during such a period, your efforts will probably be somewhat frustrated: it is very difficult to go 180 degrees against the current of atmospheric flow.

On the other hand, if you do want to do some intensive studying, what would be an ideal time of day of year? Late night or deep winter, when it is quiet outside and there is very little disturbance; it is much easier to be alone then, to quiet down your body and emphasize the energies of your brain and nervous system to become more sensitive to the world of images, deep thought, and ideas. When your number is in the north position (1 Water in the standard map), that is a more ideal time for study and philosophical self-reflection. If you try to pursue very busy social activi-

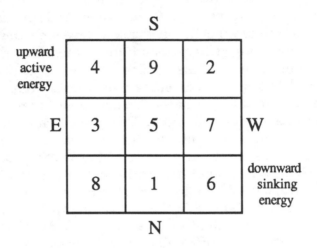

Figure 26: Movement of Heaven and Earth's Forces through the Standard Table

ties during this time, it will be more difficult than usual.

Applying this principle, you can figure out what kind of energy is coming to you when your number is in the other positions, east (3 Tree), southeast (4 Tree), southwest (2 Soil), west (7 Metal), northwest (6 Metal) and northeast (8 Soil). East, for example, represents rapid growth, new initiatives, and unexpected change. When you are occupying the east position, you may also have a slightly greater tendency to develop liver or gall bladder problems. West relates to the time of harvest and beginning of fall, a time of reaping rewards and consolidating gains, also involving a tendency toward lung or large intestine problems.

The standard table shows the type of energy that characterizes each of the nine numbers and their "home" positions. We can divide the table into two sections, corresponding to the movement of energy through the daily and yearly cycle. During the morning, rising energy generated by the earth's rotation becomes strong, creating upward movement in the atmosphere. The numbers 3 and 4 correspond to this rising, upward energy, as does spring and the positions east and southeast. Expansive, rising energy reaches its most active peak around midday, corresponding to the number 9, summer, and the direction south. In the afternoon and evening, heaven's descending energy becomes stronger, and the atmosphere becomes more quiet and condensed. The numbers 7 and 6 correspond to this more yang energy, as does autumn and the positions west and northwest. The energy of these numbers is opposite to that of 3 and 4. Then, downward energy becomes strongest at night, and this time corresponds to the number 1, the direction north, and the winter season. The energy of the 1 position is opposite to that of number 9.

The numbers 8 and 2 represent times of transition. The number 8 is positioned in the northeast and corresponds to the period when night changes into day and late winter changes into early spring. Opposite to that is the number 2 which is located in the southwest. This number corresponds to the period of transition between midday and afternoon and late summer and early autumn. The number 5 is located in the center and represents the balancing point or pivot around which the other eight numbers, energies, seasons, times of day, and positions revolve.

The energy characteristics of the nine numbers and standard positions are presented in *Figure 27*. Below we discuss each position in more detail, and offer a general view of what to expect during years when your number enters each position.

North – 1 Water – Floating or Darkness: This position corresponds to midnight when atmospheric energy is at its lowest point. When your number is in this position it is a good time for mental and spiritual development but not so

4 – Preparation	9 – Brightness	2 – Stagnation
3 – Rising	5 – Up & Down	7 – Joy
8 – Revolution	1 – Darkness	6 – Prosperity

Figure 27: Energy Characteristics of the Nine Star Ki Positions and Numbers in the Standard Table

good for outward social progress. You can use this opportunity to reflect on the past and make plans for the future. It is difficult to develop new projects during this period, so keep your expectations moderate and proceed cautiously. You may get caught up in many small details this year. Your health need not suffer, provided you are careful with your diet and are not excessive. Eating less and avoiding excessively yin foods can help you adapt successfully. An old sickness could possibly reappear during the year, and you need to be careful of extreme cold. Be careful around water. If you travel during this year, be cautious and don't exceed your capacity. During this year you may experience difficulty with love and relationships. Problems in this area are often caused by others. Relationships that were previously smooth may become clouded, and your intentions can easily be misunderstood. If you are careless, the results could be damaging. Mistakes made during this period can cause life-long regret.

Southwest – 2 Soil – Stagnation: This position corresponds to the transition from midday to afternoon, especially around 2 p.m. Atmospheric energy becomes still and quiet at this time. When your number moves to this position the slowing down of outward social progress that began in the previous year continues, although your outlook will probably brighten somewhat. Listening to the advice of others and acting conservatively can help you pass through the year successfully. This is not a good year to begin a new business or enterprise, but is better for strengthening your friendships and for study and self-development. Your financial situation may be stagnant until the latter part of the year. If you are careful about eating and drinking and conserve your energy, your health can improve. This year may be one of uncertainty in love and romance. You need to be careful about food poisoning, accidents near water, and the possibility of developing a fever, infection, or skin condition during the summer.

East – 3 Tree – Rising or Proceeding: The east corresponds to sunrise and early morning. When your number moves to this position, your destiny is bright and active. You can advance freely and the road seems clear for active progress. This is the time to accomplish your goals and ambitions, so it is important to act quickly. It is a good year to travel or start a new business. In order to be successful, be flexible, optimistic, and modest when pursuing your goals. Don't eat or drink excessively, and watch out for liver troubles, as well as trouble with your nervous system. Be careful of accidents. Love and romance tend to be active, and a new relationship may start. It is important to proceed steadily in order to avoid possible conflict. Eating less in the morning can help you realize your ambitions.

Southeast – 4 Tree – Preparation: This position corresponds to mid-morning and late spring. Your outlook is generally bright and this is a good time for achieving success. Things that were started in the previous year now begin to grow, develop, and prosper. It is better to follow through on these developments than it is to begin completely new ventures or change your focus or direction. Haste or impulsiveness can lead to trouble, so avoid doing things that you are not familiar with. It is generally a good year for your health, but care must be taken to avoid bronchitis, throat and speech problems, and trouble in the lungs, liver, and digestive organs. There is also a tendency to develop nervousness and irritability. How you manage your health during this year governs your condition for the nine years that follow. Relationships that were started previously have a tendency to develop and flourish, and this is a good year for establishing trust and harmony with others. Try to avoid eating overly salty or heavy animal foods during this time.

Center – 5 Soil – Up and Down: This position represents the balancing point between heaven and earth. When your number arrives here both positive and negative things move toward you. Therefore, it is important to be cautious and to avoid drastic changes, for example, starting a new enterprise, moving to a new location, or taking a long trip. This is not the best time for starting new ventures. It is better to stay within your capacity and heed the advice of others. Try to keep your schedule well organized.

Things tend to go smoothly during the first half of the year, while obstacles often appear during the second half. Patience and flexibility can help you pass through difficulties more smoothly, while haste and short temper may lead to further problems. In regard to health, you may experience ups and downs, and need to guard against colds, blood diseases, bronchitis, and traffic accidents. Be especially careful around high places. The tendency this year is to experience both positive and negative aspects of love and romance. If you act aggressively, the negative aspects will become more predominant. You may have an unexpected encounter with someone from your past. Foods with naturally sweet flavors, such as squash, cabbage, onions, and carrots help stabilize your condition during this period.

Northwest – 6 Metal – Prosperity: The northwest corresponds to evening and autumn. When your number moves to this position, it is time to harvest the rewards of your previous activities. You can confidently follow your natural desires this year. Your financial position may improve and your enterprises become successful. Try to avoid overconfidence or dishonesty. Be careful when borrowing or lending money. Stay within your capacity and manage your resources well. It is generally a good year for your health; however, you may be prone to exhaustion. If your lifestyle becomes irregular, and you eat and drink excessively, you risk damaging your health, the results of which can last for some time. If trouble appears, take corrective action by resting and eating and chewing well. You may also be prone to mental fatigue, as well as insomnia and heart trouble. Be careful of accidents. It is important to have good friends with whom you can talk. This can be a good year for self-development if you listen to and heed other people's advice.

West – 7 Metal – Joy: This position corresponds to the time of sunset when atmospheric energy becomes quiet and settled. When your number is in this position your efforts usually bear fruit and things tend to go smoothly. You may receive good news and gain new friendships, together with material and mental satisfaction. It is not a good year for doing unfamiliar things, but is better for maintaining activities and patterns that have already been established. Your financial situation could improve, and this is generally a good year for your health, but be careful during the changing of the seasons. You may be prone to lung and respiratory disorders, heart, kidney, or liver trouble, neurosis, or stress. It is a good year to take care of your teeth. Your relationships with the opposite sex could lead to jealousy so keep your approach modest.

Northeast – 8 Soil – Change or Revolution: This position corresponds to the time between midnight and sunrise and represents the pivot or balancing point between night and day. It is a time of change and revolution, during which you may change your living place, occupation, or way of thinking, and is the beginning of a new nine-year cycle. You may find new meaning in your life and work. This year may not be the best financially, although if you are careful, it need not be too bad. You may gain a new understanding of health and your way of eating may undergo a transformation. It is important to exercise and be physically active. You may be prone to constipation, problems with blood pressure, and mental fatigue. In love and romance, this year is a turning point during which you have the opportunity to clear up frustrations from the past. If you are successful, the future can be bright. If you act egocentrically, you may experience difficulties during the nine years that follow.

South – 9 Fire – Brightness: This position corresponds to noon or midday, and is the point of extreme brightness. It is generally a good year; however, it is important to guard against extremes that could lead to difficulties. When your number moves to this position you may receive good news. It is generally an active time in which your relationships with others are positive and you are able to do what you want to. However, in order to be successful, it is important to act from a firm base. You may have many new ideas but need to be clear and orderly when carrying them out. Try to avoid being wishy-washy or chaotic. Be careful of your blood pressure, nervous and circulatory condition, and of infectious diseases. Be cautious around fire. Your love life may flourish, but avoid superficial entanglements. You may experience trouble with your long-term relationships if you behave too emotionally.

Daily, Monthly, and Yearly Cycles

Now, suppose your number is in the south position;

you are now very active and outgoing. If you are a number 9 Fire person, this is very natural for you, and if you are a 3 or 4 Tree or 2, 5, or 8 Soil, fire nature is very close to yours. Again, it is not too unusual for you to be in this position. But if you are a number 1 Water, ordinarily you are counteracting fire types of energy; and if you are a 6 or 7 Metal person, this kind of energy tends to counteract you. One, 6, and 7 people therefore are particularly "out of their element" when in the 9 or south position. Accordingly, they should be a little cautious, as their judgment may be a little less clear than usual, and they could create some kind of accident of illness or other unintentional difficulty for themselves.

In the same way, 9 Fire and 3 or 4 Tree people should be cautious when they are in the 6 or 7 Metal positions; 2, 5, or 8 Soil and 9 Fire people should be cautious when in the 1 Water position; all three Soil and 6 and 7 Metal people should be careful when in the 3 or 4 Tree position; and both 3 and 4 Tree and 1 Water should exercise extra caution when in the 2, 5, or 8 Soil positions. More simply speaking, every person should naturally be a little wary when their energy passes through the opposite types of stages in the earth's atmospheric flow.

It is also important to realize that the daily, monthly, and yearly cycles are all a little different in their effects on us. The cycle of daily ki change, or the movement of the atmosphere over nine-day periods, mainly influences our activity among and relation to our family and close friends. The monthly change of atmosphere influences us more in the sphere of our immediate community, including our business activities, general social activities and local or regional involvements. The Nine Star Ki of the year is a global, large-scale influence, affecting our relationship to humanity as a whole. Naturally, the smaller the circle of acquaintance, the more quickly our position among those people changes: you and your wife or husband may argue and then make up on a daily basis (or even several times a day!), while your community affairs tend to move in slower circles, and your global affairs move most apparently in large circles of many months. This is not a rigid classification, however. The daily ki change also affects everyone on the earth, and such large-scale events can move very quickly at times. But you can consider these three levels of activity for practical use of the Nine Star Ki map.

Now, please take a few minutes to follow the course of your number through the various ki maps of the past nine months and past nine years, and see if you can understand the influences of those various positions and how they have affected your life. You can consider at which times you were trying to be more social or more solitary, at what times you tried to initiate new projects like the fresh growth of spring and at what times you tended to settle into past patterns and gather your energy; and see, according to your ki map position at the time, whether each activity was successful or unsuccessful. If you follow this back in some detail you can begin to apply this to the future as you plan out what activities you would like to pursue over the next several months and years.

Directionology

The basic principle of directionology is simply yin and yang. Suppose your marriage is becoming a little unstable, and you decide to take your wife on a three-month vacation to bring you closer together. So, you decide to go to the Caribbean. In the beginning it is very nice, but after five or six weeks, it grows less interesting. You start to disagree and argue, and after the full three months, you find yourself coming back alone. Why did this happen? Because you chose to go south.

As you already know, earth's centrifugal force is stronger closer to the equator, which means toward the south (in the Northern Hemisphere). Centrifugal force causes expansion, diffusion, and differentiation; also, tropical plants grow taller and are generally more yin. So naturally, you tend to separate when you suddenly move there. The north is opposite; more highly charged by heaven's yang, centripetal force coming down from the northern sky. This

91

causes a movement towards gathering and getting together. In cold weather you always want to get closer together. Staying in the north would have made it easier to solve the problem of separation.

If you look at history, you will discover that northern groups can much more easily conquer groups lying to the south than vice versa (this would be reversed in the Southern Hemisphere). It is very difficult to conquer from south to north.

		Toward 5	Opposite 5	Toward Your Number	Opposite Your Number
1	Water	N	S	NW	SE
2	Soil	N	S	W	E
3	Tree	N	S	NE	SW
4	Tree	N	S	S	N
5	Soil	N	S	N	S
6	Metal	N	S	SW	NE
7	Metal	N	S	E	W
8	Soil	N	S	SE	NW
9	Fire	N	S	Center	Center

Figure 28: Unfavorable Directions During 1991

Also, it is difficult to conquer from west to east, but relatively easy to conquer from east to west. Why is this? Here you must consider the direction of the earth's rotation, which runs west to east. Because of this, the earth's atmosphere, the influence of the sun, and the current of heaven's force showering down through the region of the north pole, all travel in the opposite direction, from east to west.

Ancient people said that it is very difficult to conquer the world if you go against the sun (west to east). Hitler and Napoleon both attempted world conquests in this direction and failed. Alexander the Great also suffered defeat in this direction. On the other hand, when Europeans came west to America, they were successful and became materially very powerful. Even if you take a plane trip from America to Europe, it takes about one day's rest to catch up, while on the return trip this is often unnecessary.

Because of these two principles, it is often very easy for a northeastern area to rule an entire region, just as New England functioned as the leader of the United States for so long, and is in many ways still doing so. Japan occupies a similar position in relation to much of Asia, while Germany has also been very influential and materially powerful in relation to Western Europe.

This is the basic principle of directionology: when you change from one location to another, it may be easier to adapt to that new environment or more difficult to adapt; depending on that factor, your trip will be comparatively successful or unsuccessful. At the same time, of course, atmospheric energy is always moving, so the relative ease or difficulty of adapting to different areas changes as well. After thousands of years of experimenting, ancient people concluded that there are four generally dangerous directions of travel:

• **In the Direction of Number 5** – They call this *Go O Satsu* or "Five Yellow Killing." During the time of any given ki map, it is best to avoid traveling in the direction occupied by the number 5. During 1991, for example, when 5 is in the north, traveling in that direction will tend to be difficult. If you go this way, you may experience some kind of misfortune such as an accident while traveling, or once you have arrived, you may become sick, have financial difficulties, or be unsuccessful in your purpose for going.

• **In the Opposite Direction from Number 5** – This is known as *An Ken Satsu* or "Dark Sword Killing." The meaning of "dark sword" is this: if you travel toward number 5, you will have some very clear, direct, obvious misfortune, while if you travel in the opposite direction, you will tend to suffer from more subtle or unexpected kinds of misfortune, symbolized by a sword coming at you out of the darkness. You could say, these are the yang aspect and yin aspect of number 5 danger.

• **In the Direction of Your Own Number** – This is called *Hon Mei Satsu* or "Self Life Killing." Whatever position your number occupies, try to avoid traveling in that direction.

• **In the Opposite Direction from Your Own Number** – This is known as *Teki Satsu* or "Target Killing."

If your number is in the center, as you already know, it is best to avoid travel altogether, and if the number 5 itself is in the center, it is best for everyone to stay put, using that day, month, or year to develop themselves, reflect, stabilize, and prepare for the future. In other words, when number 5 occupies the center, all travel as a whole is somewhat more risky than usual, especially for a number 5 Yellow Soil person. In *Figure 28* we present examples of unfavorable directions for travel during 1991. You can use this chart as well as the Nine Ki maps of the years from 1990 to 2000 to see what yearly directions are unfavorable during the 1990s. You can use the monthly ki maps in *Figure 25* to calculate unfavorable directions for the months of 1991 and beyond.

Steps to Minimize Danger in Travel

Practically speaking, you may often find you have to travel in unfavorable directions. When this happens, you should check both the year and the month: if that direction is dangerous within one map, but generally safe within the other map, then you can go ahead, only exercising a little extra caution. If both the month and the year are unfavorable for the particular travel direction, then you can at least choose a day which is more favorable.

If you must travel in a dangerous direction, another way to minimize that danger is to go and come back within two weeks: this means you will be traveling in both directions within the same half-cycle of the moon. In that case it is easier to keep your condition strong and your judgment clear. Short trips are preferable to long trips as is moving within the same latitude. Actually changing your address and moving permanently is very difficult if the year and month are not favorable; usually you will find that you eventually move back again, unable to accomplish what you had tried to do with that move. If the year indicates a dangerous direction, it may take 2 or 2 1/2 years before you reestablish equilibrium; until then, you will tend to experience great frustrations and failures.

In addition, there are three steps you can take to avoid or minimize this type of danger in traveling:

• **Bring a Companion** – Take someone with you for whose sign this is not a dangerous direction of travel. Even better, have that person make all the arrangements: let her choose the time of leaving, the exact travel route and method, and take the lead when you go (you can just follow and carry the luggage). Since her energy nature is not counteracted by the present atmospheric flow, her judgment will be clearer and you will more easily avoid delays, mistakes, and errors in intuition that could cause accidents.

• **Change Your Travel Route** – Rather than moving directly and suddenly to the new environment, plan a more indirect route that will take you to your destination by way of several less dangerous directions. For example, if you are going southwest, say from Boston to Los Angeles, you can stop first in San Francisco and then proceed south to Los

Angeles. You can also go down to Miami and then fly due west. In this way, you can cushion the effects of the change in environments and acclimatize your condition to the new atmospheric conditions.

• **Change Your Diet** – For three or four days before your trip, you can begin to eat in a way that harmonizes more with the environment of your destination. If you are moving, for example, from a fairly cool, dry place to a damp, warm climate, you can spend several days eating a little more summer style of food, including more salad or lightly cooked food, a little less salt, and so forth. In other words, instead of waiting until you get there to eat that local type of food and cooking, begin now, and you will already be better adjusted once you arrive.

This third method, however, is very difficult unless you are already eating generally good food. If you are eating dairy food, fatty food or any oily, floury food, even though you may crave certain adjustment types of foods and begin eating according to that new climate, your condition will not react quickly. For quick, immediate adjustment of your condition, you have to be very clean and balanced.

When your condition is good you can anticipate every single danger or opportunity with your intuition – and interestingly enough, if your intuition is working well it works exactly this way. In other words, this Nine Star Ki map is not an arbitrary invention or artificial creation of intellectual minds, but is actually a map of the way ki is moving, which the biological, spiritual faculty of human intuition can also detect.

When you are eating well and feeling very clear, then you intuitively know what directions and what activities or initiatives are dangerous or auspicious, without having to check different charts. The best way is to use both; first use you intuition to make your decision, then check out how well that correlates with what you have learned, and then try it out and see how it actually happens.

Directionology in Relationships

Although we already studied human relations and how to judge your compatibility with other people, your day to day changing relationships to other people can also be followed by using the Nine Star Ki map principle.

Suppose you want to approach a certain person to establish some kind of new tie; maybe you want to propose marriage, initiate some new business venture, or collaborate with that person on some kind of project. Before you approach, first check the ki map for that month, and see what position that person's number occupies; if that is a dangerous direction for you to travel, there will be a tendency for your judgment to be cloudier than usual when you contact that person, and your project may fail or begin on a shaky foundation. In that case, it might be wiser to wait for a more favorable month.

Let's take an example: suppose you are a number 6 Metal, and you want to do business with a number 8 Soil person; the month is number 2. Checking on the ki map for a number 2 month (shown in *Figure 25*), you find that 8 is in the southwest, opposite to number 5: this is the Dark Sword Killing direction; in fact, it is not so favorable for anybody to approach number 8 people with new plans for this month. However, that person can very safely and easily approach you: you are in the south, which is a perfectly fine direction for a number 8 person to travel in the month.

So, if you go ahead and make your move, it is more than likely that you will not fare so well in the outcome of your project, but the other person may do quite well. If you wait until the next month, which would be a number 1 Water, the situation is reversed: your approach to number 8 (travel to the east) is perfectly safe and auspicious, while the number 8 person would have to move to the Dark Sword Killing direction (now in the north) to approach you. If you wait until this month to take the initiative, you will probably experience the opposite outcome from the previous month.

If you decide to wait until the next month, which would be number 9 Fire, both directions will be free of danger; either of you can safely approach the other. This would be an excellent time to establish your new partnership.

If the two of you are both the same number, and therefore always occupying the same position, then approaching each other is at the same time always favorable and always unfavorable! In other words, there is always some special risk involved, and there is also always very favorable potential involved. Since you are the same sign, you are very similar: you can understand and cooperate with each other well, yet there is also a certain natural tendency to repel each other.

Although earlier I suggested that you regard the season of birth as determining a person's second nature, the number corresponding to the birth month also has some influence on a person's character. This is somewhat more subtle and deeper than the influence of the birth season, which is quite external and clear. However, in the case of children, this birth month number is very important: until a person passes through adolescence, the character of the birth month may be much in evidence. Since they are still rapidly growing, their conditions are still going through more rapid changes than for adults. During this time, you can use the number of the birth month as representing the child's primary character; this is particularly true for younger children and infants.

You may have already figured out that approaching a number 5 Yellow Soil person always means moving in a dangerous direction: *Go O Satsu* or "Five Yellow Killing" is always towards the position that number 5 occupies. Actually, it is true: there is always some risk in approaching a number 5 person! This is the one type that does not correlate to a trigram, the most stable, balanced type; because of this, one is always at something of a disadvantage in the company of a number 5 Soil, since every other type is somewhat imbalanced in relation to them. Although 3 and

4 Tree people have somewhat more of an advantage than others, it is always wise to use some caution when entering into a new relationship with a number 5 person and to realize that they will to some degree tend to be in control of the situation!

Planetary Destiny

Every sixty years the two cycles of heavenly influence (*Ten Kan*) and earthly influence (*Twelve Shi*) coincide and synchronize with a new cycle beginning in the same year. These sixty-year periods alternate, one having a generally more yin tendency and the next being overall more yang. The combination of a more yin sixty-year period and a more yang sixty-year period gives us one large cycle of 120 years; this 120-year cycle marks major epochs of human destiny.

Specifically, the *Ten Kan* cycle begins with Tree Elder Brother, or *Ki No E*, which represents the fresh, new energy of early spring. Within the cycle of *Twelve Shi*, the Year of the Rat corresponds to this same energy. The last time we saw a Rat year and Elder Brother Tree year occurring in the same year was in 1984: this marked the beginning of a new epoch for humanity.

Around the time of an epoch change such as 1984, major celestial events usually arise, together with dramatic changes in various aspects of human affairs. At the same time, the 120-year period between 1984 and 2104 is itself the end of a much larger cycle, the 25,800-year cycle representing the shifting influence of the constellations over the north pole, or cycle of the ecliptic. As we discuss in some detail in *The Book of Macrobiotics, One Peaceful World, Other Dimensions,* and other books, the star Polaris will come directly overhead in about the year A.D. 2100, ushering in a completely new era with the opposite tendencies from our present era, an Age of Humanity that will emphasize spirituality over material development, and worldwide cooperation as opposed to territorial gain.

In addition, it will be at this time that the progression of

Nine Star Ki year energy shifts from the present Yang *Ton*, or descending process, to the ascending process of Yin *Ton*. The years themselves will begin to progress in order from 1 to 9 (as the days do every year during the spring and early summer). Accordingly, the pace of life will gradually begin to reverse, moving more and more calmly and peacefully, and an age of peace will gradually be established, lasting for another 10,000 years.

This particular 120-year period, in other words, represents the conclusion of over 12,000 years of yang, material development and will involve a tremendous transition process. The 1990s will see this change of direction accelerate as we move further into that last 120-year transitional period.

As we enter this period, we can also use the Nine Star Ki understanding to see what general tendencies each year and month will manifest, to help us guide our efforts in making this transition as smooth as possible.

As you already know, the general tendency of this time is one of degeneration: we can see this in the form of cellular degeneration, such as AIDS, cancer, diabetes, multiple sclerosis, and other diseases; as social degeneration, such as the decomposition of marriages, families, and communities; as mental and intellectual degeneration, institutional degeneration, economic, political, cultural, and spiritual degeneration, and in many other forms. At the same time, a new current of rebirth, solidification, and recovery is emerging out of this pattern, represented by what we are presently calling macrobiotics.

However, these general tendencies change every year and indeed every month and every day. There are also larger Nine Ki cycles that last 9 and 81 years. These cycles affect the character of each period and have a broader, more pervasive influence than yearly or monthly cycles. Below we consider how these larger cycles influence world events, and particularly the way in which they are helping to shape the transition toward a new spiritual civilization.

The 81-Year Cycle

Every 81 years, the earth's atmosphere assumes a certain pattern of movement that corresponds to one of the nine numbers and stages of energy. As it does in the yearly and monthly cycles, the energy in this larger cycle moves downward from 9 to 1. The 81-year cycle gives a certain character to a span of time that lasts for several generations.

The current 81-year cycle began in 1955 and will last until 2036. During this period, the number 9 occupies the center of the chart. We are currently in an 81-year epoch that has the characteristics of a Nine Purple Fire Year, during which the general movement of society tends to reflect the rapidly expanding and diffusing tendency of fire nature. This high energy period is governed by strong centrifugal force, and until it ends, many of the institutions and ways of thinking established during the previous cycle will collapse.

1955-2036

8	4	6
7	9	2
3	5	1

Figure 29: Nine Star Ki Map for the 81-Year Cycle from 1955-2036

Fire nature creates the tendency toward high speed and the intense use of energy. Under this influence, instantaneous electronic communication, chemicalized food and agriculture, nuclear missiles, atomic energy, fast food, high speed transportation, food irradiation, home computers and fax machines, and microwave ovens have developed and spread around the world. Fire energy also imparts an unstable and rapidly shifting character to society.

The previous 81-year cycle was governed by 1 Water. The Nine Ki map for that period corresponded to that of a 1 Water year. During that period, which ended in 1955, the number 5 occupied the south position. Within society, the energy of 5 Soil creates the tendency toward centralization and control, as well as war and conflict. During that era, political power was centralized in the hands of a few people, and entire populations mobilized around a central issue or person. That period saw the rise of dictatorships and the consolidation of state control, along with two World Wars. In the 9 Fire epoch that we are now in, the number 5 has moved to the north. Its influence lies dormant, as if in deep winter, and thus it has become far more difficult for any one individual or group to accumulate vast political or economic power.

Recent events in Eastern Europe and the Soviet Union are examples of this 9 Fire tendency. The centralized Soviet system established during the 1 Water epoch is now in the process of coming apart. Individuals and groups that were once incorporated into that huge centralized system are no longer united by a single ideology and are now seeking independence and self-determination. That movement actually started soon after Stalin's death in the early 1950s and coincided with the change from a 1 Water to a 9 Fire epoch. In liberal societies, this tendency manifests itself in such things as the fragmentation of politics into numerous competing special interests and the failure of any single issue or cause to override the others and unite large numbers of people.

During the 9 Fire epoch, we have also seen a continuous acceleration in the rate of biological and psychological degeneration, and that trend will continue into the immediate future. The spread of AIDS and other viral diseases offers an example. By the year 2005, there could be as many as 12.5 million cases of AIDS in the United States, with roughly 5 percent of the population affected. By that time, the number of people infected with HIV could approach one quarter of the population, or about five times the number of actual cases. If HIV continues spreading, by 2010, 50 percent of the population could be infected, while by 2030, practically the entire population could be harboring the virus.

The increasing incidence of cancer offers another example. Despite one hundred years of scientific research and the expenditure of billions of dollars, the rate of cancer has increased substantially. In the 1800s, cancer was a rare disease, while today it is commonplace and affects every family. Below are the increases in the incidence of cancer that have occurred in the United States in the twentieth centu-

Year	Proportion of U.S. Population
1900	1 out of 25
1950	1 out of 8
1985	1 out of 3
Future Projections	
2000	1 out of 2
2020	4 out of 5
2030	virtually everyone

Figure 30: The Increasing Incidence of Cancer in the United States

ry, along with future projections based on these levels.

During the present 81-year cycle, heart and cardiovascular disorders have become epidemic. In terms of energy, the heart and circulatory system correspond to active fire nature. They are particularly sensitive to extremes and imbalances during a 9 Fire period. Moreover, society itself is showing signs of unraveling. The family is on the verge of collapse, with the number of divorces approaching 50 percent of all marriages, while biosocial problems, including crime and drug abuse, have also reached epidemic proportions.

Any one of these destructive trends has the potential to destroy modern civilization. The convergence of so many at once makes it unlikely that civilization will continue in its present form beyond the next century. The rise in medical costs alone could bankrupt modern society. Driven by the decline in personal health, medical expenditures in the U.S. currently consume 12 percent of the Gross National Product, double the proportion consumed by national defense. Unless medical spending is restrained, medical costs will eat up the entire GNP by the middle of the next century, according to one estimates.

These trends will continue until a new era begins in the year 2036. At that time, an 81-year cycle during which 8 Soil occupies the center will begin. As we saw, 8 Soil corresponds to early morning around 2 a.m.: the time during which night changes into day. An 8 Soil period is a time of change or revolution. During the next epoch, many of the concepts and systems of our present civilization will be discarded, and planning for a new civilization will start actively. New concepts of economy, government, medicine, science, and society will emerge and be implemented, leading eventually to the establishment of a peaceful planetary culture.

Our era is one of preparation for this new time. To pass through this period, we must change ourselves from the inside, by changing the quality of our blood, cells, body, and consciousness. Artificial or partial approaches cannot stop the overall trend toward personal and social degeneration. Moreover, any attempt to force conformity or control will inevitably lead to conflict and chaos. Modern systems are of no use in the recovery of genuine health and consciousness. What is needed is an understanding of natural law and a way to apply this understanding in daily life. The understanding and practice of each individual is the key point, as is the dissemination of clear information that will enable each person to gain that understanding. Regardless of the difficulties that arise in future, a new current is emerging based on the recovery of natural health and consciousness. During this 81-year period, this new current will gather force, emerge as the leading edge of civilization, and guide humanity into a new era.

Predictions for the 1990s

The 1990s have the potential to be a time of great possibilities and equally great dangers. Based on the study of the Nine Star Ki and the repeating cycle of twelve yearly energies, there are more potentially dangerous years in the decade between 1990 and 2000 than there were in any of the previous decades of the 20th century.

The 1990s will be governed by a nine-year cycle in which the number 5 occupies the central position. Nine-year cycles occur within the larger 81-year cycle and also correspond to the nine basic energies. A new nine-year cycle with 5 in the center began on February 4, 1991, and will last until February 3, 2000. During the cycle that began in 1982, the number 6 occupied the center. The directional maps for both of these cycles are shown in *Figure 31*.

Nine Star Ki can help clarify the way in which these cycles influence the movements of society. Each domain of human activity corresponds to a stage of energy in the Nine Star Ki. The basis for this classification is the division of various activities into yin and yang. For example, things such as art, music, and entertainment are manifestations of upward, outgoing energy and correspond to the yin transformations tree and fire. Activities such as law, finance, and government are based on coordination and control and governed by downward, consolidating energy. They correspond more to the the transformations soil and metal. More precise correspondences between the nine numbers and various spheres of social activity are presented in *Figure 32*.

1982-1991

5	1	3
4	6	8
9	2	7

1991-2000

4	9	2
3	5	7
8	1	6

Figure 31: Ki Maps for the Nine-Year Cycles
1982-1991 and 1991-2000

On the whole the transformations soil and metal represent more condensed, materializing energy, while tree and fire represent more upward, expressive, and expansive energy. During the nine-year cycle that began in 1982, 6 Metal was in the center. Because of the central dominance of 6 Metal, the 1980s were governed by a materialistic trend in which activities like banking, finance, and the stock market were the center of attention. The idealism of earlier times gave way to the cold realities of profit and loss and to a "get-rich-quick mentality." The 80s were a decade of corporate mergers, junk bonds, leveraged buy-outs, huge trade deficits, multilevel marketing schemes, inflated real estate prices, *The Art of the Deal*, and "yuppies." Politics also reflected this trend. Liberalism, for example, is a product of

Air Travel, trade and commerce	Art, music, entertainment, news and public events, fashion	Agriculture, food production, education
4	9	2
Technology, invention, electronic communication	Government and politics	Management and Organization
3	5	7
Ideas, research, soicial "isms," planning	Restaurants and public eating places, ground transportation	Banking, financing, investment
8	1	6

Figure 32: Social Characteristics
According to Nine Star Ki

the more upward, expansive, and idealistic energy created by tree and fire nature. Conservatism is governed by the more consolidating influence of soil and metal. During the 1980s, the public turned conservative, as personalities like Margaret Thatcher and Ronald Reagan took center stage. World attention also focused on Mikhail Gorbachev, a 6 Metal personality who was born in 1931 (a 6 Metal year). By 1989, *Time* magazine had named Gorbachev "Man of the Decade."

With 2 Soil in the north during most of the decade, it was a difficult time for education and agriculture. Tax cuts, a huge defense buildup, and massive federal deficits left many educational institutions without adequate funding. (Many macrobiotic educational centers also had a difficult time financially.) Agriculture, also represented by 2 Soil, entered a period of low energy and stagnation. Many farmers struggled economically, and agricultural output declined as the result of several droughts.

Trade and commerce, represented by 4 Tree, were very active during the decade. (Four Tree was in the east; a position of high energy and activity.) Japan, for example, pursued an aggressive policy of exporting cars and consumer goods and captured large shares of the global market. As a result, the United States and other countries accumulated huge trade deficits with Japan, and the United States went from being the world's largest creditor to the world's largest debtor. Japanese corporations also invested in banks, factories, and real estate in America and other parts of the world.

As we can see in *Figure 32*, the energy of 5 Soil corresponds to government and politics. In 1989 (a 2 Soil year), the number 5 moved to the northeast (occupied in the standard table by 8 Soil.) This is the position of change or revolution, and it was during that year that revolutionary changes occurred in the communist governments of Eastern Europe and the Soviet Union. These changes led to the fall of the Berlin wall and the reunification of the two Germanies.

The 1980s saw sexually transmitted diseases emerge as a major public health concern. In 1982, *Time* magazine did a cover story on the herpes epidemic, and stated that 30 million Americans were carrying the herpes virus. Soon afterward, another sexually transmitted disease, AIDS, captured public attention and reached epidemic proportions throughout the world. The energy of 1 Water corresponds to the sexual organs. During the 1980s, 1 was in the south (a position of maximum activity and high energy) and was governed by a rapidly diffusing, expanding energy characteristic of the rapid spread of virus diseases. Interestingly, the number 1 also corresponds to restaurants and public eating places. During the 1980s, this energy was especially active, and fast food and eating out became a daily way of life for many people.

Many of these trends will change during the 1990s. Government and politics, which correspond to 5 Soil, will replace banking, finance, and investment as the central focus of attention. With each of the numbers in its home position for most of the decade, each domain of social activity will revert to its own native character. In ideal circumstances, each segment of society supports the center during a period such as this and develops according to its nature. However, when circumstances are not ideal, the negative aspects generated by each number converge at the center and weaken it. The 1990s have the potential to be a decade of either great unity, stability, and growth, or great disunity, chaos, and decline.

The global wars of the 20th-century broke out during 5 Soil periods. World War I started in 1914; World War II became global in 1941; and the Korean War broke out in 1950: all 5 Soil years. In this next nine-year period, the number 5 will move to the center of the chart and the danger of large-scale war will intensify. This danger will be particularly acute in years during which 5 occupies the center of the yearly cycle, or during years when the energy of 5 Soil is particularly active. Looking at the yearly maps for the 1990s in *Figure 24*, we see that the year 1995 will be a 5 Yellow Soil Year. In this year, society will experience a double 5 effect, with a 5 Soil year occurring in the middle of a 5 Soil nine-year cycle. If war breaks out in that year, it will have the tendency to be on a world scale. This influence will be moderated somewhat by the position of 5 Soil in the north during the entire 81-year period from 1955-2036. (North is the position of inactive, dormant energy similar to that of deep winter.) When 5 moved to the north in 1955, the world entered the era of nuclear stalemate. At that time the notion of global war went from "hot" to "cold," and the idea of the "Cold War" began.

During this nine-year cycle, as well as during the year 1995, 9 Fire will occupy its home position in the south. Fire energy will be very active, and this creates the tendency for conflicts to spread rapidly across a large area and not stay limited to one place. Other potentially dangerous years in this decade include 1990 (5 in the south), 1993 (5 in the east), 1994 (5 in the southeast), and 1999 (5 in the south). In these years the number 5 will be in the most actively energized of the nine positions. Periods of lesser, but still some, danger include 1992, 1996, 1997, and 1998. They are dangerous because of the convergence of activating energy from the twelve-year cycle on the numbers 5 and 9, both of which relate to the potential for destructive war. In 1991, the energy of 9 Fire also creates the potential for explosive conflict, and as we can see, the danger of war is present during each year of the decade.

The current crisis in the Middle East broke out in 1990, a 1 Water year in which 5 Soil was in the south, an especially high-energy position. The Middle East is also a 9 Fire region, and with 5 in the south – the home base of 9 Fire – it was predictable that a crisis involving the massing of armies and the possibility of war would occur there. Even if the immediate crisis between the United States and Iraq eases and war is averted, we can expect an even greater crisis to develop unless the respective countries fundamentally alter their way of life, especially their way of eating. For example, energy savings brought on by even modest reductions in meat consumption in the United States could eliminate the need to import oil from the Middle East, and thus help diffuse the crisis. The modern diet of meat, sugar, and hot spices is potentially explosive, especially in a hot, dry climate. The fanaticism of some leaders in this part of the world, however, is matched by the obstinancy of Western rulers, whose thinking and behavior have also rigidified because of excess animal food and been dulled by dairy. Unless these factors change, a Middle Eastern war leading to global conflict is a very real possibility in the 1990s.

The energy that causes major earthquakes will also be active during the 1990s. Earthquakes are triggered by 3 Tree energy. During the 1991-2000 cycle, 3 Tree will be in its home position in the east. This is an especially active position represented by the upward energy of morning, and the possibility of major earthquakes will intensify during this nine-year period. Then, if we follow the movement of the number 3 through the yearly maps of the 1990s (shown in *Figure 24*), we can see when this energy will be especially active, and thus when the probability of large-scale earthquakes is greatest. The most active years for 3 Tree energy are 1992 (3 Tree in the south), 1994 (3 Tree in the southwest), 1995 (3 Tree in the east), 1996 (3 Tree in the southeast), and 1997 (3 Tree in the center).

Whether or not we are able to successfully pass through difficulties such as these depends on our health, thinking, and intuition. If these factors are sound, potential dangers can be minimized. If they are unsound, potential dangers become greater.

Personal and Planetary Health

Nine Star Ki can help clarify the relationship between personal health and society. As shown in *Figure 33*, each of the body's regions corresponds to one of the energies and numbers of the Nine Star Ki. The head, for example, corresponds to 9 Fire. The brain generates thoughts and images that have a more yin, diffused, and invisible nature that corresponds to fire energy. The lower body, including the region of the sexual organs, has an opposite tendency and corresponds to the downward, floating energy of 1 Water. The reproductive organs create new life that develops in an inward, contracting spiral that is opposite to the spiral of mental and spiritual activity centered in the head. Reproductive cells are also typical of the primitive life that evolved billions of years ago in a moist, watery environment. The mouth and digestive system also correspond to water energy. Digestion is a process in which foods are mixed with digestive liquids and broken down into a primitive form.

Clear thinking and spiritual insight are indications that the 9 Fire aspects of a person's constitution are strong and well balanced. However, in the modern world, a variety of mental disorders, including Alzheimer's disease, affect millions of people. Instead of being strong and well developed, these 9 Fire factors are declining rapidly. Moreover, drug and alcohol abuse, both of which are widespread today, also impair brain function and thinking ability. The condition

111

Number	Energy	Region of body and Corresponding Functions	Common Dysfunctions
9	Fire	Head and thinking ability	Mental illness. Alzheimer's disease, Arthritis, multiple, sclerosis, muscular dystrophy, variouscrippling disorders
8	Soil	Left leg	Hepatitis, liver cancer, gallstones
7	Metal	Right side of the body, including the liver and gallbladder and their functions	Sciatica, arthritis, various crippling diseases
6	Metal	Right leg	Arthritis, tension, lack of perseverance
5	Soil	Center of the body, including the pancreas, kidneys and their functions	Pancreatic cancer, hypoglycemia, diabetes, kidney stones, kidney failure
4	Tree	Left arm and perseverance	Arthritis, tension, lack of perseverance
3	Tree	Left side of body, including the spleen and lymph system	Lymphoma, Hodgkin's disease, weaking of natural immunity,
2	Soil	Right arm and ability to do work	Arthritis, physical weakness, and inability to work
1	Water	Mouth and digestive system sexual organs and reproductive ability	Digestive disorders, prostate enlargement and cancer, infertility, sexually transmitted diseases, gynecological problems

Figure 33:   The Nine Energies and Regions of the Body

112

of these individual factors in turn influences the corresponding social factors shown in *Figure 32*. When these individual factors are strong and well developed among people in general – art, music, and fashion elevate humanity and inspire spiritual insight and clarity. When these individual factors decline, these forms of human expression also decline and begin to reflect a strange, deluded view of reality.

The right and left arms and shoulders correspond to the ability to do work, including the vitality and perseverance necessary for activities such as farming, food production, and manufacturing. They correspond to the social factors represented by 2 Soil and 4 Tree respectively. When these individual factors are strong and active among the population, society can prosper and become secure. However, today increasing numbers of people have become physically weaker than their predecessors. A shockingly high percentage of American children are overweight and unable to per form minimum tests of strength and endurance. At the same time, disorders such as arthritis, multiple sclerosis, and other crippling diseases have become increasingly widespread. The prevalence of these conditions, coupled with the overall trend toward declining physical vitality and a growing disinclination to work hard, impacts on the areas of society that correspond to these numbers and energies. In the United States, declining productivity caused by declining personal health has led to a situation in which America is in danger of losing its leading position in the world economy.

When each of the individual 9 Ki factors is strong and well balanced in the population as a whole, society can maintain and develop the systems it has created. As these factors become weak, as they are now doing, the corresponding areas of society will also weaken and change. As physical and mental health decline in the 1990s, modern social systems will become increasingly unstable.

Seeing Destiny in the Face

As we can see in *Figure 34*, the regions of the face correspond to the energies and numbers of the Nine Star Ki. The middle forehead, for example, corresponds to 9 Fire energy, while the nose and area immediately around it correspond to the energy of 5 Soil. Each region, in turn, reveals the general outline of a person's destiny during the corresponding year in the Nine Ki cycle. The center of the forehead, therefore, reveals our overall destiny during 1991, a 9 Fire year, while the nose shows our potential outlook for 1995, a 5 Soil year. These correspondences are shown in the diagram.

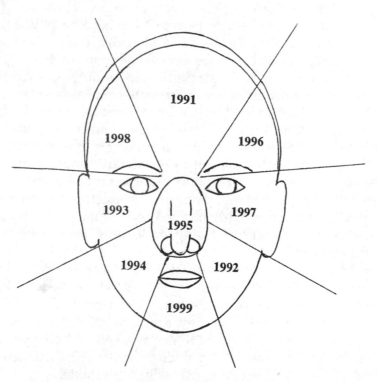

Figure 34: Nine Star Ki Years and Corresponding
Regions of the Face

A bright, clear color in each area shows that a person's destiny during the corresponding year is generally bright and positive. A light yellow or pink coloration also reveals the potential for good fortune. On the other hand, a dark, greyish, bluish, bright red, green, or purple shading indicates potential misfortune in the corresponding year. Moles, freckles, or scars in a particular area also reveal potential misfortune. Our facial characteristics and the destiny they reveal are simply reflections of our present condition. By changing our daily diet and way of life, we can alter these characteristics and change potential misfortune into potential good fortune.

Toward One Peaceful World

Each of the Nine Ki numbers will be in its home position within the standard table for the next nine years, while also changing position from year to year, and during this time people will have the tendency to think and act in harmony with their native character. The key to passing successfully through this time lies in developing the strengths of your particular Nine Ki character, while minimizing the negative aspects. Health is the key to bringing forth the positive potential of each number and character. Modesty, or the avoidance of extremes in our eating, thinking, and lifestyle can help us pass through difficulties while steadily developing our dream of health and peace.

The different aspects of individual human life correlate with the nine numbers and energies, as shown in *Figure 35*. The key to changing all of these factors in a positive way lies in changing the factors represented by the three soil numbers. The energy of 8 Soil corresponds to our hopes, dreams, and wishes for the future; 2 Soil to our daily way of eating; and 5 Soil to our health, wholeness, and existence itself. By eating well, developing a dream of a health and peace, and orienting our life in harmony with nature and the universe, we can positively influence all of the other aspects of our existence. The three soil factors are therefore basic and are the key to changing not only our personal des-

Words and Expressions 4	Spirit 9	Food 2
Thoughts and Images 3	Health and Existence 5	Body 7
Wishes, Hopes, & Dreams 8	Sex and Human Relations 1	Breathing 6

Figure 35: The Nine Star Aspects of Human Life

tiny, but the destiny of the entire planet.

In the 1990s, the movement toward natural health, world peace, and ecological harmony will spread throughout the world, despite the dangers posed by war, earthquakes, and the collapse of modern insitutions and ways of thinking. The final decade of the 20th century represents a turning point: the end of an era characterized by increasing-separation from nature and our true selves, and the beginning of a new world based on health, peace, and harmony with our planetary environment.

In the Ki Flow

by Gale Jack

Dear Gale,
Many people are worried about another drought this summer. According to Oriental astrology, what will the weather be like? — Parched in Topeka

Dear Parched,
1989 is a 2 Soil year, so that atmospheric conditions will generally be more stable and orderly than last year. Six Metal governs the summer, so it should be very yang — active, condensed, continued dry and hot. However, June and July should be slightly wetter than usual, and September more unsettled.

Dear Gale,
My boyfriend (a 9 Fire) has job difficulties and doesn't want to get married until these are resolved. I'm a 3 Tree. Should I wait or put down roots somewhere else? — Stranded in San Diego

Dear Stranded,
His inability to commit is from an overly yin condition. (Yang makes commitment.) The question is whether he's

---

These questions and answers originally appeared in Gale's column, "In the Ki Flow," in the One Peaceful World Newsletter.

eating your cooking? If he is living with you or nearby, eating your cooking at least once a day, and has some understanding of yin and yang, his condition will gradually improve. In that case, you can be patient. If not, there is little chance for your relationship and you should branch out elsewhere.

Dear Gale,
    I recently sold my condo and am thinking of investing in the stock market. Is the time right? — **Going for It in Miami Beach**

Dear Going for It,
    To invest in the stock market is always risky. There could be a great gain or loss. Better is to invest in your dreams such as some holsitic or spiriutal enterprise. Since this is a 2 Soil year, food quality will be at the center of things (note the Alar pesticide scare and the tainted Chilean fruit this year). You will have more control over the outcome of a natural foods store than, say, stock in Exxon. Besides, it contributes to your own self-sufficiency and a healthier world. That way, even if you lose materially, you will gain spiritually.

Dear Gale,
    What's the best time for a tonsillectomy? — **Anxious in Arkansas**

Dear Anxious,
    Chronically swollen tonsils are the body's way of telling you that you are taking too much yin, especially fruits, juices, soft drinks, ice cream or other fatty, mucousy foods. You may notice that many tonsillectomies are given in July or August, because of excess consumption of these foods when the weather starts to warm up. Taking your tonsils out will eliminate symptoms and discomfort, but drive imbalance deeper into the body. Better than taking your tonsils out is putting good food in.

Dear Gale,

My wife of ten years suddenly wants to separate and live in Florida. What should I do? — Alone in St. Paul

Dear Alone,

Often the expansiveness of summer, as well as eating more yin foods, leads to separation, while cold and more balanced foods bring people together. Be patient and see how things go when the snows start falling.

Dear Gale,

We're thinking of opening a new natural foods store. Would autumn be a good time? — Setting Up in Sunny California

Dear Setting Up,

This September and October will be more active months because Tree Energy will be in the center of the ki flow. In contrast, November and December will be quieter as the atmospheric energy changes to the Soil and Water positions. Tree energy is ideal for starting new ventures.

Dear Gale,

Whan you talk about the months in Nine Star Ki, do you go by the ordinary calendar? — Confused in Nova Scotia

Dear Confused,

The ki flow changes several days into the calendar month. It is often marked by observable changes in the weather or atmosphere, such as rain, storm, or break in the temeprature. This autumn the ki flow changes on Oct. 8, Nov. 7, and Dec. 7. Watch for changes on these days.

Resources

Studies in Destiny — In these ongoing seminars presented at the Kushi Institute of the Berkshires, Michio Kushi explores many of the topics discussed in this book. Included are fascinating and revealing studies of the way to see, judge, and freely manage your personal destiny — and the destiny of planet Earth — based on yin and yang, the *I Ching*, Nine Star Ki and Oriental astrology, and the art of physiognomy. These residential seminars include macrobiotic/vegetarian meals.

Spiritual Training Seminars — These ongoing seminars presented at the Kushi Institute of the Berkshires, are part of a progressive series designed to enhance each person's capacity for self-realization anf fulfillment. They feature practice and experience and include studies of reincarnation and the spiritual world, *The Gospel According to Thomas*, the teachings and prophecies of Buddha, Jesus, and Nostradamus, as well as meditation, prayer, and chanting for health and peace. Spiritual Training Seminars are presented by Michio Kushi and feature simple macrobiotic/vegetarian meals.

For information about these and other macrobiotic resources and programs, contact:

The Kushi Institute
Box 7
Becket, Mass. 01223
(413) 623-5742

One Peaceful World — One Peaceful World is an international information network and friendship society of macrobiotic friends, families, educational centers, organic farmers, traditional food producers, teachers and parents, authors and artists, publishers and business people, and other individuals and organizations around the world devoted to the realization of one healthy, peaceful world. Activities include educational and spiritual tours, assemblies and forums, international food and agricultural projects, the One Peaceful World Village and Children's Memorial and Shrine in Becket, the quarterly *One Peaceful World Newsletter* and other communications.

For membership information and a current catalog of publications and videos, contact:

One Peaceful World
Box 10
Becket, Mass. 01223
(413) 623-5742

For Further Study

Michio Kushi has authored and inspired a wide variety of books that deal with topics such as those presented in this publication. The following titles are especially recommended for further study. Those with an asterisk include material on Nine Star Ki.

1. *The Book of Macrobiotics* (with Alex Jack), Tokyo and New York: Japan Publictions, 1986.*

2. *One Peaceful World* (with Alex Jack), New York: St Martin's Press, 1986.*

3. *Other Dimensions: Exploring the Unexplained* (with Edward Esko), Garden City Park, N.Y.: Avery Publishing Group, 1991.*

4. *Food Governs Your Destiny: The Teachings of Namboku Mizuno* (with Aveline Kushi and Alex Jack), Tokyo and New York: Japan Publications, 1991.*

5. *Macrobiotic Palm Healing: Energy at Your Fingertips* (with Olivia Oredson), Tokyo and New York: Japan Publications, 1989.

6. *The Book of Do-In*, Tokyo and New York: Japan Publications, 1979.

7. *The Gentle Art of Making Love: Macrobiotics in Love and Sexuality* (with Edward and Wendy Esko), Garden City Park, N.Y.: Avery Publishing Group, 1990.

8. *Macrobiotics and Oriental Medicine* (with Phillip Janetta), Tokyo and New York: Japan Publications, 1991.

9. *On the Greater View: Collected Thoughts on Macrobiotics and Humanity* (with Sherman Goldman), Garden City Park, N.Y.: Avery Publishing Group, 1987.

10. *The Cancer-Prevention Diet* (with Alex Jack), New York: St. Martin's Press, 1983.

11. *Diet for a Strong Heart* (with Alex Jack), New York: St. Martin's Press, 1985.

12. *Promenade Home: Macrobiotics and Women's Health* by Gale and Alex Jack, Tokyo and New York: Japan Publications, 1988.*

13. *AIDS, Macrobiotics, and Natural Immunity* (with Martha Cottrell, M.D.), Tokyo and New York, Japan Publications, 1990.

14. *Natural Healing Through Macrobiotics* (with Edward Esko and Marc Van Cauwenberghe, M.D.), Tokyo and New York: Japan Publications, 1979.

15. *How to See Your Health: The Book of Oriental Diagnosis*, Tokyo and New York: Japan Publications, 1980.

16. *Macrobiotic Home Remedies* (with Marc Van Cauwenberghe, M.D.), Tokyo and New York: Japan Publications, 1985.

17. *The Macrobiotic Approach to Cancer* (with Edward Esko), Garden City Park, N.Y.: Avery Publishing Group, 1991.

18. *The Macrobiotic Way* (with Stephen Blauer), Garden City Park, N.Y.: Avery Publishing Group, 1985.

About the Authors

Michio Kushi was born in Kokawa, Wakayama-ken, Japan, in 1926 (a 2 Soil year) and devoted his early years to the study of international law at Tokyo University. Following World War II, he became interested in world peace through world government and met Yukikazu Sakurazawa (known in the West as George Ohsawa), who had revised and reintroduced the principles of Oriental philosophy and medicine under the name macrobiotics. Inspired by Ohsawa's teaching, he began his lifelong application of traditional macrobiotic thinking to modern world problems.

In 1949, Michio Kushi came to the United States to pursue graduate studies at Columbia University. Since that time, he has lived in this country and lectured throughout the United States, Canada, Eastern and Western Europe, Japan and other parts of Asia, Australia, and South America. He is the founder of Erewhon, a pioneer distributor of natural foods, the *East West Journal*, a monthly magazine dealing with alternative lifestyles and holistic health, and the *Order of the Universe*, a journal of philosophy and science. In 1978, he founded the Kushi Institute, an educational center for the training of macrobiotic teachers and health counselors headquartered in western Massachusetts, with affiliates throughout the world. Michio Kushi has published a number of bestselling books, including *The Book of Macrobiotics*, *The Cancer-Prevention Diet*, *The Macrobiotic Way*, and *One Peaceful World*. He currently lives in Brookline and Becket, Massachusetts, with his wife, Aveline (a 5 Soil), also a leading voice in macrobiotic education. His ongoing activities are reported in the quarterly newsletter, *One Peaceful World*.

Edward Esko, a 5 Soil, helped pioneer macrobiotic education in North America during the 1970s. He began studies with Michio Kushi in 1971 and for the last seventeen years has taught macrobiotic philosophy, health care, and related subjects throughout the United States and Canada, as well as in Western and Eastern Europe, South America, and Japan. He has lectured on modern health issues at the United Nations in New York and is on the faculty of the Kushi Institute of the Berkshires. He has co-authored or edited several popular books including *Natural Healing through Macrobiotics, Doctors Look at Macrobiotics, The Gentle Art of Making Love,* and *Other Dimensions.* He lives with his wife, Wendy (a 6 Metal), and seven children in Becket, Massachusetts.

Gale Jack, a 7 Metal, teaches cooking, health care, and Nine Star Ki at the Kushi Institute of the Berkshires. Her autobiography, *Promenade Home,* describes her life as a mother, elementary school teacher, psychological counselor, and macrobiotic cook in her native Texas. She lives with her husband, Alex (a 1 Water), in Becket, Massachusetts.

Index

*Additional copies of this book
are available from:
One Peaceful World Press
P.O. Box 10
Becket, Massachusetts 01223*